MATH

MADE SIMPLE

Portable Press
An imprint of Printers Row Publishing Group
10350 Barnes Canyon Road, Suite 100, San Diego, CA 92121
www.portablepress.com • mail@portablepress.com

Copyright © 2020 Quarto Publishing plc

Correspondence regarding the content of this book should be sent to Portable Press, Editorial Department, at the above address. Author, illustration, and rights inquiries should be sent to Quarto Publishing plc, 6 Blundell Street, London, N7 9BH, www.quartoknows.com.

Portable Press
Publisher: Peter Norton • Associate Publisher: Ana Parker
Senior Developmental Editor: April Graham Farr
Editor: Angela Garcia

Produced by The Bright Press, an imprint of Quarto Publishing plc
Publisher: James Evans
Editorial Director: Isheeta Mustafi
Managing Editor: Jacqui Sayers
Editors: Katie Crous and Abbie Sharman
Art Director: Katherine Radcliffe
Designers: Tall Tree and Subtract Design
Cover Design: Greg Stalley
Cover Images: Shutterstock

Library of Congress Cataloging-in-Publication data available on request.
ISBN: 978-1-64517-253-6

Printed in China

24 23 22 21 20   1 2 3 4 5

MATH

MADE SIMPLE

A COMPLETE
GUIDE IN TEN
EASY LESSONS

KATE LUCKETT

PORTABLE
PRESS

San Diego, California

CONTENTS

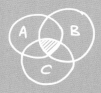

INTRODUCTION

Math helps us make sense of the world around us; it can provide order in the chaos. Through learning math skills, we also gain the power of reasoning, thinking creatively to understand spatial ideas, and being able to think critically about things. The most important skill we obtain from practicing math is the ability to solve problems systematically—this is the core of mathematics.

Math Made Simple spans the fundamental topics, such as **simple calculations**, to more complex topics, such as **probabilities and statistics**. This book will introduce you to key terms and symbols in a fun way with entertaining examples, and with each concept thoroughly explained. In every chapter, you will discover how that topic is useful when applied to science, art, or nature, for example. Furthermore, there are **spot quizzes** in each section and **short quizzes** at the end of most lessons, so you can test your progress.

The early chapters cover topics on **basic numbers and arithmetic**. While these sections may appear simple for some, they are useful when making sure you have a good fundamental knowledge base upon which to build. Many people struggle when they have gaps in this knowledge base: it is crucial to fill in these gaps, to be able to progress and understand more complex theories.

Once this knowledge base is built, the book moves on to more **complex calculations** and working with more complicated types of numbers: decimals, fractions, and measurement units. Then, through the use of interesting and detailed examples, often based on real-world scenarios, you will be able to understand how to convert between measurement systems, identify and describe **2-D and 3-D shapes**, and use angle rules to solve geometry problems.

This leads to the chapter on **algebra**, one of the most misunderstood but very useful subjects in math. Algebra helps us solve problems more quickly and reinforces logical thinking, while forming the basis for statistics (which you will encounter later). Lastly, you will see that algebra is used to describe, in basic form, real-world phenomena such as Einstein's Theory of Relativity, or the laws of gravity.

Math is not always about calculations—it includes **presentation of data**. In Lesson 9, you will discover the plethora of ways to present information, so that others can understand it better, sometimes in simple forms such as tables or more complex graphs. In the last lesson, we look beyond just practicing and learning **concepts** to where these concepts came from and how they are used in the world today.

This guide is designed to make these concepts accessible to everyone who is willing to learn and to show just how interesting math can be. From avid mathematicians to the math-averse, this book will help develop your ability to problem-solve and **shape the world around you**, therefore making it the most useful subject to understand.

ABOUT THIS BOOK

This guide of **10 lessons** (chapters) is designed to start off simply, and covers core concepts slowly, thereby introducing the key cornerstones of math. It is recommended that you go through the book lesson by lesson, in order, as each chapter builds in some way on the ones before it. However, if something doesn't make sense, try and move on to see if the following topics help develop your understanding.

- **LESSON INTRODUCTION**
At the start of each lesson is a handy introduction, to outline the key learning points.

FACT Most topics have an intriguing fact highlighted in an easy-to-see box.

QUIZ TIME

Find these quizzes at the end of each chapter and grade yourself on your understanding and progress before moving on to the next lesson.

SIMPLE SUMMARY

At the end of each chapter is a summary, to help you recap on the topics covered.

ANSWER THIS

At the end of most topics is a spot test, which should help to assess whether you have fully understood the information on those pages and how to apply it in real-life situations. Earlier topics are often used as parts of examples, which will help build your skills. Try to answer these questions immediately after reading the relevant pages, without peeking at the text for the answers.

- **ANSWERS**
Turn to the back of the book for answers to all the Answer This and Quiz Time tests—no peeking, now!

1

NUMBERS: THE BUILDING BLOCKS

Numbers are the fundamental building blocks of math, so knowing how to work with them and the different types is a vital skill. This chapter will cover how to effectively read and write numbers, how to convert very big and very small numbers in a different form, and how to estimate effectively. It will also introduce you to some key types of numbers.

WHAT YOU WILL LEARN

Numbers and order

Negative numbers

Decimals

Standard form

Rounding and estimation

Bounds

Factors, multiples, and primes

Square and cube numbers

NUMBERS AND ORDER

Numbers are everywhere. Whether it's looking at the bus schedule, finding the cost of concert tickets, or counting the likes on social media posts, numbers are ever present and tell us vital information. Count the number of times you encounter or need to use numbers in a day; you may be shocked.

Numbers are a way of communicating amounts of things. From a young age we learn to count to 10, usually with fun colored blocks. This enables us to tell someone else how many items there are. The basic order of 1–10 is learned and then the groupings: putting tens in the second position to the left; hundreds in the third position; thousands in the fourth position, and so on. Grouping numbers by tens or hundreds allows us to write numbers clearly, so they are easily and quickly understood.

However, numbers haven't always been so easy to understand. Modern numbers are much clearer than numerals used by the Romans—1999 is much clearer than MCMXCIX. The beauty of modern numbers, and the standardized way in which they are ordered, is that they convey information quickly and effectively.

> **FACT**
>
> Numbers are used almost everywhere in modern life; however, there are a small group of people for whom numbers are not incredibly important. The Pirahã tribe in the Amazon do not have numbers greater than two; they only have words for "one," "two," and "many." The word for "one" is the same as "small."

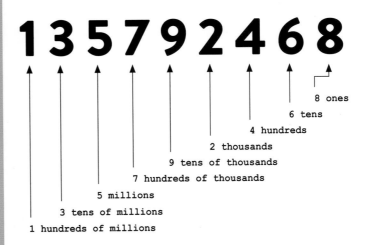

135792468

8 ones
6 tens
4 hundreds
2 thousands
9 tens of thousands
7 hundreds of thousands
5 millions
3 tens of millions
1 hundreds of millions

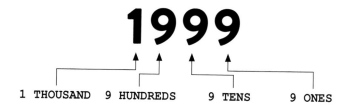

1 THOUSAND 9 HUNDREDS 9 TENS 9 ONES

Special numbers

Certain numbers have their own special labels: integers, evens, odds, primes, squares, roots (some are covered later). An integer is a whole number, for example 3. If a number is even, it can be halved (divided by two) and results in an integer, e.g., 8 divided by 2 is 4. When an odd number is halved, the result is not an integer, e.g., 7 divided by 2 equals 3.5.

Ordering numbers

When you have lots of separate numbers, it can be useful to order them by size. This is called ranking. Numbers can be ordered in one of two ways: ascending or descending. Ascending numbers go from smallest to largest; descending numbers go from largest to smallest. This gets a little more complicated when ranking decimal numbers, but that's covered later (see page 16). By ranking ages in your street, for example, you could quickly see the youngest, oldest, and most common ages.

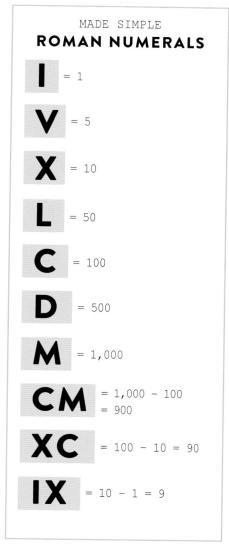

MADE SIMPLE
ROMAN NUMERALS

I = 1

V = 5

X = 10

L = 50

C = 100

D = 500

M = 1,000

CM = 1,000 − 100 = 900

XC = 100 − 10 = 90

IX = 10 − 1 = 9

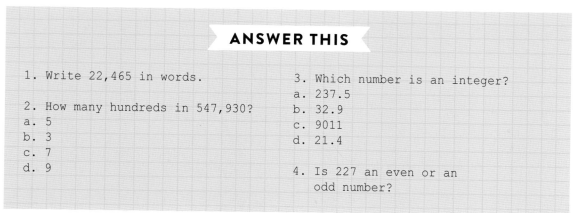

ANSWER THIS

1. Write 22,465 in words.

2. How many hundreds in 547,930?
a. 5
b. 3
c. 7
d. 9

3. Which number is an integer?
a. 237.5
b. 32.9
c. 9011
d. 21.4

4. Is 227 an even or an odd number?

NEGATIVE NUMBERS

Numbers less than zero are called negative numbers and they have a minus sign (-) in front of them. Negative numbers can be found on bank statements to show money is owed, on the stock market to show a decrease in value, or on a temperature scale to show that it's cold. They are not always a bad thing, however, as in golf, when a negative number means better than the average number of strokes, or par.

Numbers less than zero are negative; numbers greater than zero are positive; zero is neither negative nor positive. Negative numbers can be hard to get your head around, so using a number line is useful. When adding numbers to a negative number, count to the right; when subtracting from a negative number, count to the left (away from zero). The further right along the number line you go, the higher the number; the further left, the lower

---

MADE SIMPLE
ADDING OR SUBTRACTING NEGATIVE NUMBERS

There are two rules to follow when adding or subtracting a negative number:

1. When adding a negative number, count to the left (the number should be smaller).

2. When subtracting a negative number, count to the right (the number should be bigger).

NUMBER LINE

-10 -9 -8 -7 -6 -5 -4 -3 -2 -1 0

To add 5 to -3, count five spaces
to the right, landing on 2.

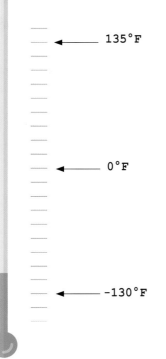

°F

THERMOMETER

← 135°F

← 0°F

← -130°F

the number. So -20 is lower than -2, despite 20 being bigger than 2, but it is further along to the left, away from zero.

Temperature changes

One of the most common things we measure that includes negative numbers is temperature. Often, we look at rises or drops in temperature, and a number line can be helpful again. For example, James bought a new freezer for his restaurant and the rules state such freezers must be kept at 0°F or less, meaning negative numbers (numbers less than 0) are fine. When he plugged it in, it was registering 20°F; when he took the temperature the next day it was -2°F. Marking both the temperatures on the line and then counting how many degrees are between them shows that the freezer temperature decreased by 22°F.

ANSWER THIS

1. Which is the lowest number?
a. 10
b. -22
c. -10
d. 36

2. -4 + 2 =
a. -2
b. -6
c. 6
d. 2

3. -10 - 3 =
a. -7
b. 7
c. -10
d. -13

1 2 3 4 5 6 7 8 9 10

To subtract 5 from -3, count five spaces to the left, landing on -8.

DECIMALS: WHAT'S THE POINT?

Decimal numbers contain whole numbers and part of a whole number. A point, known as a decimal point, is seen between the whole number and the fraction, or part. These fractions, or parts, are written in tenths, hundredths, thousandths, and so on.

In the numbers section, we saw that as you move away from the ones column it went up in tens, hundreds, thousands, and tens of thousands. In the same way, as you move away from the ones in decimal numbers, it goes down in tenths, hundredths, etc.

Putting decimal numbers in ascending or descending order can be tricky and often people get it wrong. Many individuals think the smallest number is the one with fewest digits after the decimal point; this is not usually the case.

MADE SIMPLE
DIGIT COLUMNS
Table of digit columns on each side of the decimal point

Thousands	Hundreds	Tens	Ones	Decimal	Tenths	Hundredths	Thousandths
4	3	2	1	•	2	3	4

FACT

In fast-paced sports like Formula 1, the results can come down to the hundredth of a second. Rubens Barrichello beat Michael Schumacher to win the 2002 United States Grand Prix by only 0.011 seconds.

USA 2002 GRAND PRIX RESULT

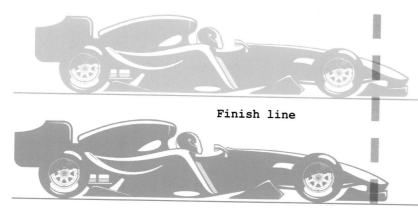

1:31:07.934

RUBENS BARRICHELLO

Finish line

+ 0.011

MICHAEL SCHUMACHER

For example, during the school's field day, six students jump the long jump. Their jumps are as follows: 1.78 m, 1.692 m, 1.7 m, 1.71 m, 1.69 m, 1.764 m. We want to put the jumps in order so we can identify the shortest and longest. The common mistake would be to put 1.7 m as the smallest, as it has the fewest digits.

The first thing to do is add zeros on the end of the numbers, so they have the same number of digits. Our longest number has three digits after the decimal point, so they are now: 1.780 m, 1.692 m, 1.700 m, 1.710 m, 1.690 m, 1.764 m.

They all have the same ones digit, so that doesn't help us, but there are two with 6 as the tenths digit and 9 in the hundredth digit. To decide which one goes first, we have to look at the thousandths digit: 2 is bigger than 0, therefore 1.690 m must be before 1.692 m.

That now covers all numbers with 1.6 at the beginning, so we move on to 1.7. It is best to scratch out numbers as you put them in order, so you don't leave any out. As the remaining numbers all have 7 in the tenths position, we look at the hundredths: 1.700 m is less than 1.710 m, which is less than 1.764 m, which is less than 1.780 m.

Final order: 1.69 m, 1.692 m, 1.7 m, 1.71 m, 1.764 m, 1.78 m.

1.4 STANDARD FORM

When dealing with very big or very small numbers, it can be easy to write them incorrectly or miscalculate them. Standard form helps by providing a standard way of writing these numbers. For example, the distance from the Earth to the Sun is 149,600,000,000 meters, which can be written as 1.496×10^{11} m. Or, for very small numbers, such as the size of a bacterial cell, 0.00000005 m is the equivalent of 5×10^{-8} m.

Standard form has a very specific format with three key rules. The format is illustrated below: N is a number between 1 and 10, but it must be less than 10. Another way to write that is $1 \leq N < 10$. The power, or index, of 10, shown as "y" in the expression, is how far the decimal point moves; y is a positive for large numbers and a negative for small numbers.

MADE SIMPLE

HOW TO WRITE NUMBERS IN STANDARD FORM

$$N \times 10^y$$

When converting big numbers into standard form, we have to identify the front number first then count how many times the decimal will move. For example, there are an estimated 37,200,000,000,000 cells in the human body, and we want to convert this to standard form. The front number (N in the illustration) must be between 1 and 10, so it becomes 3.72. The decimal has moved 13 places to the left and so the number becomes 3.72×10^{13}.

 FACT When the Hubble telescope was first launched, it sent back blurry images. Unfortunately, they found that when the primary mirror was manufactured it was 1×10^{-6} m too flat; the surface was not curved enough.

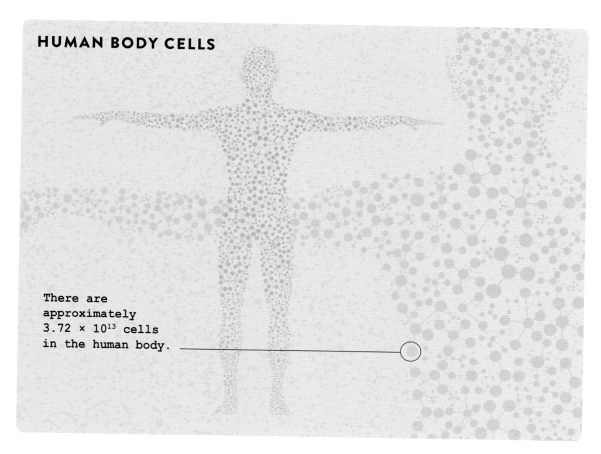

HUMAN BODY CELLS

There are approximately 3.72×10^{13} cells in the human body.

When converting small numbers into standard form, we use a negative index. The approximate weight of a human cell (in kg) is 0.000000000001. To convert this to standard form, take the first number that isn't zero (luckily, in this example it is 1) and use that as the front number: 1. Then count how many times the decimal point would move to leave the 1 on the left: 12. As the decimal was moving to the right, this becomes -12, so the number becomes 1×10^{-12} kg.

Ordering numbers in standard form

If you have a mix of numbers written in standard form and "normal" numbers, then first convert them all to standard form. You can now tell from the index how big the numbers are: if the index is positive, then the larger the index, the larger the number; if the index is negative, then the smaller the index, the larger the number.

ANSWER THIS

Convert the following into standard form:
1. 2,000
2. 57,210,000
3. 0.00004
4. 0.00000000692

ROUNDING AND ESTIMATION

Have you ever wondered why numbers are rounded off? Rounding numbers simplifies them and makes them easier to use in calculations. Rounded numbers are, however, less accurate, and are considered an estimation of the actual value. If exact numbers aren't required, it's often easier to work with rounded numbers.

Rounding off a number simplifies the number, so calculations are easier. Rounding off numbers can be confusing, depending on the level at which you are asked to round. Numbers are often rounded to the nearest ten, hundred, thousand, or just the nearest whole number if it has a decimal or fraction part.

In rounding, there are two important numbers: the "key" number and the "deciding" number. The key number is the level you are rounding to. For example, if we take the number 187,426 and want to round to the nearest ten, 2 is in the tens column and this is the key number. The number immediately right of the key number is the deciding number, in this example, it is 6.

FACT

Rounding numbers is often used in budgets to account for unknown amounts. We may not know exactly how much the builders will cost for the extension, but can estimate; it's best to round this up so you know you have enough money!

CALCULATION

The calculation of

$$460 \times 29$$

can be rounded to

$$500 \times 30$$

which is easier.

Calculations can be made easier by rounding numbers; however, this is only an estimate.

MADE SIMPLE
RULES: ROUNDING

There are two rules for rounding numbers:

1. If the deciding number is less than 5, then the key number stays the same.

2. If the deciding number is greater than or equal to 5, then the key number is rounded up by 1.

In our example, the deciding number is 6, therefore greater than 5, so we round up the key number of 2 to 3, and the final number is 187,430, to the nearest ten.

Rounding decimals follows the same process, however, instead of rounding to tenths, hundredths, etc., you round to a decimal place. The decimal place is the number of digits after the decimal point; so, for example, in 8.354 the digit 4 is in the third decimal place.

If we want to round 4.901 to two decimal places, the digit in the second decimal place is the key number: 0. The deciding number is, therefore, in the third decimal place: 1. Revisiting the rules above, 1 is less than 5, so the key number remains the same: 4.90.

ANSWER THIS

1. Round 1,985,640 to the nearest million:
   a. 1,000,000
   b. 2,000,000
   c. 1,990,000
   d. 1,985,700

2. Round 770 to the nearest hundred:
   a. 800
   b. 700
   c. 750
   d. 850

3. Round 11.5 to the nearest whole number:
   a. 12
   b. 11
   c. 11.9
   d. 10

4. Round 11.086 to two decimal places:
   a. 11.1
   b. 11.08
   c. 11.087
   d. 11.09

BOUNDS: ERRORS IN ROUNDING

When you round numbers, they are no longer accurate, and therefore the results of any calculations will not be exact. These answers will contain some error, and bounds are a way of taking that error into consideration. A rounded number has a lowest possible value and a highest possible value prior to rounding—these are known as the bounds.

Bounds (sometimes written as limits) are the range of values a rounded number could take before it is rounded. An upper bound is the smallest value that has been rounded up to the next value (one higher than the rounded number). A lower bound is the smallest value a rounded number could have been. For example, a length of 180 cm was rounded to the nearest 10 cm. The lower bound is 175 cm, as that is the smallest length that would round up to 180 cm. The upper bound is 185 cm, as that is the smallest length that would round up 190 cm (the next highest rounded number). This is written as follows:

175 cm ≤ length < 185 cm

So, our length can be greater than or equal to the lower, but must be less than, the upper bound (otherwise it would round up to 190 cm).

The range of values, or the bounds, are dependant on the rounding unit. The rounding unit is the level at which you are rounding to. For example, if rounding to the nearest ten, then the rounding unit is 10. Whenever a number is rounded, the original value can be up to half the rounding unit, bigger or smaller.

ANSWER THIS

1. If 2,020 has been rounded to the nearest ten, what is the upper bound?

2. If 200 has been rounded to the nearest hundred, what is the lower bound?

3. If 19 has been rounded to the nearest whole number, what are the upper and lower bounds?
   a. 19 ≤ x < 20
   b. 18 ≤ x < 20
   c. 19.5 ≤ x < 20.5
   d. 18.5 ≤ x < 19.5

It is key to remember the biggest value or the upper bound doesn't actually round to the rounded value we are given, it rounds up. That's why we write it has to be "less than" to be our rounded number.

Example

If 110 was rounded to the nearest ten, we take half of 10 (the rounding unit), which is 5, and first subtract that to the rounded number, which gives the lower bound: $110 - 5 = 105$. Second, add 5 to the rounded number, which gives the upper bound: $110 + 5 = 115$. The bounds are written as: $105 \leq x < 115$.

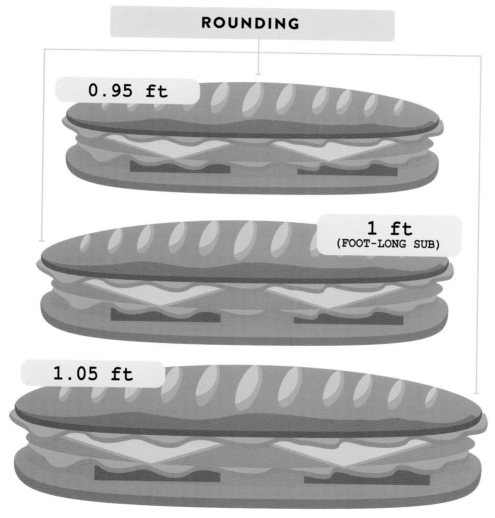

ROUNDING

0.95 ft

1 ft
(FOOT-LONG SUB)

1.05 ft

"Foot-long" sandwiches may be rounded up or down, so it could be larger or smaller than the foot they claim to be.

1.7 FACTORS, MULTIPLES, AND PRIMES

Factors of a number are all the numbers that exactly divide into it; multiples of a number are values found in the number's times tables; and primes are a whole number which only has two factors—1 and itself.

Factors of a number are whole numbers that divide exactly into the original number. For example, 5 is a factor of 20, as it divides exactly (leaves you with a whole number). To find factors, you need to go step by step from 1: if trying to find all factors of 20, start at $1 \times ? = 20$. $1 \times 20 = 20$; therefore, 1 and 20 are factors. Then go step by step through 2, 3, 4, 5, 6, and so on, until half of 20 (10).

CALCULATIONS

When trying to identify factors of a number, go through the numbers one by one to see if they multiply to get the desired number.

$1 \times 20 = 20$
$2 \times 10 = 20$
$3 \times ? = \times$
Cannot make 20 so NOT a factor
$4 \times 5 = 20$
$5 \times 4 = 20$
$6 \times ? = \times$
Cannot make 20 so NOT a factor

$7 \times ? = \times$
Cannot make 20 so NOT a factor
$8 \times ? = \times$
Cannot make 20 so NOT a factor
$9 \times ? = \times$
Cannot make 20 so NOT a factor
$10 \times 2 = 20$

 FACT Most prime numbers are odd numbers, as otherwise they can be divided by 2; in fact, 2 is the only prime number that is an even number. However, 1 is not a prime number as it only has one factor, not two.

COMMON MUTIPLES

When finding the common multiple of two numbers, write out their times tables. For example, when finding the common multiple of 3 and 8:

THREE TIMES TABLE:

3   6   9   12   15   18   21   **24**   27   30

EIGHT TIMES TABLE:

8   16   **24**   32   40   48   56   64   72   80

24 is a multiple of both **3** and **8**, as it is found in both times tables.

In this case, only 1, 2, 4, 5, 10, and 20 are factors of 20. Common factors of two numbers are values that are a factor of both numbers. For example, 5 is a common factor of both 10 and 20.

Multiples of a number are simply values in that number's times table. For example, a multiple of 5 can be 10, 15, or 20, as they are found in the five times table. Common multiples of two numbers are multiples found in both numbers' times tables. If we are looking for a common multiple of 3 and 8, we start by writing out their times tables and looking for numbers in both lists: 24 is in both the three and eight times tables, so therefore is a common multiple of 3 and 8.

Prime numbers only have two factors: themselves and 1. What that means is that a prime number can only be exactly divided by itself and 1. The first ten prime numbers are 2, 3, 5, 7, 11, 13, 17, 19, 23, and 29. Other than 2 and 5, prime numbers tend to end in 1, 3, 7, or 9, but it is important to note that not all odd numbers are prime numbers, e.g., 9 has a factor of 3, not just 1 and 9. To identify a prime number, search for all possible factors, and if it only has two—itself and 1—then it is a prime number.

ANSWER THIS

1. Find all the factors of 12.

2. What is the largest factor of 32?
   a. 16
   b. 64
   c. 1
   d. 32

3. List the first five multiples of 9.

4. What is the first common multiple of both 6 and 8?
   a. 12
   b. 24
   c. 30
   d. 48

5. Is 67 a prime number?
   a. Yes
   b. No

1.8 SQUARE AND CUBE NUMBERS

In math, a square of a number is the product of that number multiplied by itself twice. For example, 16 is a square number of 4, as 4 × 4 = 16. A cube number of a number is the product of that number multiplied by itself three times, for example, 64 is the cube number of 4, as 4 × 4 × 4 = 64. Square and cube numbers are important when looking at areas of squares and volumes of cubes.

A square number is the result of multiplying a number by itself. When we square a number, we use a small "2" next to and above the number, which is called the index: $2^2 = 2 \times 2 = 4$. When showing we are squaring a number, the index must always be a 2. The index tells us how many times that number is multiplied by itself. Square numbers are useful in working out lengths of sides of squares when you only have the area.

THE SQUARE NUMBERS

1^2	2^2	3^2	4^2	5^2	6^2	7^2	8^2	9^2	10^2
1	4	9	16	25	36	49	64	81	100

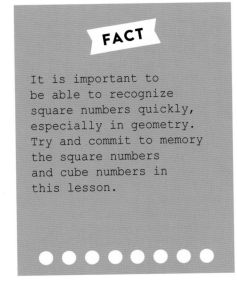

FACT

It is important to be able to recognize square numbers quickly, especially in geometry. Try and commit to memory the square numbers and cube numbers in this lesson.

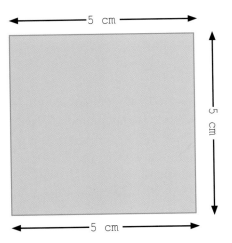

5 cm

5 cm

5 cm

5 cm

CALCULATING AREA

The area of a square with 5 cm-length sides will be 5 × 5, or 5^2, = 25 cm^2.

THE CUBE NUMBERS

1^3	2^3	3^3	4^3	5^3	6^3	7^3	8^3	9^3	10^3
1	8	27	64	125	216	343	512	729	1000

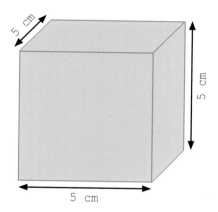

5 cm
5 cm
5 cm
5 cm

CALCULATING VOLUME
The volume of a cube with 5 cm-length sides will be 5 × 5 × 5, or 5^3, = 125 cm^3.

In a square, all the sides are the same, so to work out the area of a square, times the side by itself. This only works with squares, not other quadrilaterals. For example, to find the area of a table mat that is square, with each side 8 cm long, multiply 8 by itself, so 8 × 8, or 8^2, = 64 cm^2.

A cube number is the result of multiplying a number by itself three times: $3^3 = 3 × 3 × 3 = 27$. Cube numbers are often useful when we have the volume of a cube. The volume of a cube is worked out by multiplying the width by the length by the height; if all of those are the same, then we are just multiplying the same number by itself three times. This only works with cubes, and not with cuboids or other 3-D quadrilaterals, unfortunately. For example, to find the volume of an ice cube with sides 2 cm long, multiply the side length by itself three times: 2 × 2 × 2, or 2^3, = 8 cm^3.

1. 81 is the square number of which number?
   a. 7^2
   b. 6^2
   c. 8^2
   d. 9^2

2. What is the square number for 6^2?
   a. 49
   b. 36
   c. 30
   d. 12

3. What is the cube number for 4^3?
   a. 64
   b. 16
   c. 32
   d. 4

4. 1,000 is the cube number for which number?
   a. 10^3
   b. 9^3
   c. 1^3
   d. 100^3

NUMBERS

1. How many tens of thousands are in 32,891?

   a. 3

   b. 2

   c. 9

   d. 1

2. Put the following numbers in ascending order: 101, 132, 146, 52, 111, 113, 98, 72, 129, 99.

3. Which is the lowest number?

   a. -4

   b. -8

   c. 4

   d. -21

4. At midday, the temperature was 4°F, but once the sun went down, it dropped to -11°F. How much did the temperature drop from midday?

   a. 15°F

   b. -15°F

   c. 11°F

   d. 4°F

5. What is the value of 4 in 10.6491?

   a. Ones

   b. Tenths

   c. Hundredths

   d. Thousandths

6. Convert 6,872,000 to standard form.

7. Round 869 to the nearest hundred.

8. 7,890 has been rounded to the nearest ten, what is the lower bound?

   a. 7,900

   b. 7,899

   c. 7,880

   d. 7,885

9. Find all the factors of 24.

10. Most prime numbers end in 1, 3, 7, or 9, but is 99 a prime number?

    a. Yes

    b. No

11. What is the cube number for 5^3?

    a. 5

    b. 25

    c. 125

    d. 625

12. Fill in the blank spaces:

Number	Square number
1	1
2	4
3	
4	16
5	
6	
7	49
8	
9	
10	100
11	
12	

Answers on page 210

SIMPLE SUMMARY

Numbers tell us vital information and are a way of communicating amounts of things.

- Numbers can be ordered in one of two ways: ascending or descending.

- Numbers less than zero are negative; numbers greater than zero are positive; zero is neither negative nor positive.

- Decimal numbers contain whole numbers and part of a whole number, with a point between the two.

- Standard form provides a standard way of writing very big and very small numbers, and the format is: $N \times 10^y$.

- When rounding numbers, if the deciding number is less than 5, then the key number stays the same; if the deciding number is greater than or equal to 5, then the key number is rounded up by 1.

- Bounds are the range of values a rounded number could take before it is rounded.

- Factors of a number are all the numbers that exactly divide into it; multiples are values found in the number's times tables; and primes are a whole number which only has two factors—1 and itself.

- A square of a number is the product of that number multiplied by itself twice; a cube of a number is the product of that number multiplied by itself three times.

2

CALCULATIONS

Learning how to do basic calculations is important
to progressing in math and adopting problem-solving
skills. In this chapter, you will learn the basic arithmetic
operations you need to master—including addition,
subtraction, division, and multiplication—both with
and without a calculator.

WHAT YOU WILL LEARN

Adding and subtracting

Multiplying and dividing
without a calculator

Order of operations

Doing math in your head

Multiplying and dividing by
10s, 100s, 1000s

Calculating with money

ADDING AND SUBTRACTING

Calculations are used as a way to figure out a problem. There are four main types of calculations: adding, subtracting, multiplying, and dividing. Most of the time we use addition and subtraction, such as adding up the cost of a drink and a sandwich at lunchtime and seeing if you have enough money to cover it. The focus in this section will be on carrying out additions and subtractions on larger numbers by hand.

Addition

The sum of two numbers is found by adding (+) them together. Beyond the standard school tests, there may be a time when you don't have a calculator and you have to add two large numbers, so it is important to know how to carry out addition by hand.

When adding two numbers, the first step is to write one of the numbers above the other, lining up the ones column. It doesn't matter which number is on top. In the illustration below we add 8542 and 1271. Starting at the right, add up the numbers in each column and place the number at the bottom of that column. Sometimes the column will add up to 10 or more; write the right-hand digit in the answer space and carry the left-hand digit to the next column on the left. Add this digit to the

ADDITION

$$
\begin{array}{r} 8542 \\ +1271 \\ \hline 3 \end{array}
\qquad
\begin{array}{r} 8542 \\ +1271 \\ \hline 13 \end{array}
\qquad
\begin{array}{r} 8542 \\ +1271 \\ \hline 813 \end{array}
\qquad
\begin{array}{r} 8542 \\ +1271 \\ \hline 9813 \end{array}
$$

 1 1 1

└─ carry the 1 └─ add the 1

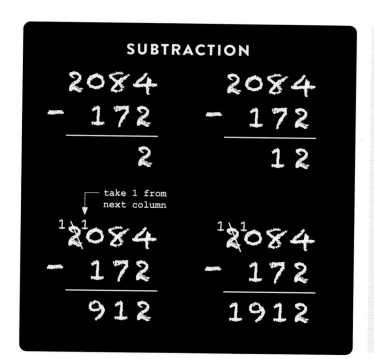

$$2084$$
$$- 172$$
$$\overline{2}$$

$$2084$$
$$- 172$$
$$\overline{12}$$

take 1 from
next column

$$^1\cancel{2}084$$
$$- 172$$
$$\overline{912}$$

$$^1\cancel{2}084$$
$$- 172$$
$$\overline{1912}$$

ANSWER THIS

1. What is the sum of 2347 and 3640?

2. 10948 + 91039 =

3. What is the difference between 4652 and 1839?

4. 845 - 265 =

5. 245 + 32 - 180 =

sum of the two numbers in the next column. This is shown step by step in the illustration, where an extra 1 had to be added to the hundreds column. Always check your answers, as simple mistakes are often made.

Subtraction
Subtraction is the difference of two or more numbers. The difference of two numbers is when one number is minused (–), or taken away, from the other. This can be slightly more complicated when done by hand.

Like addition, line up the two numbers above each other, making sure the ones column is aligned. It is very important that the number on top is the number you are subtracting from. In the illustration example above, 172 is being subtracted from 2084; therefore 2084 is on top. Minus the ones column, then the tens, and so on. Similarly to addition, it may get a bit complicated when the number on top is smaller than the one below it. In this case, take one from the column immediately to its left, so the number on top is now bigger. In really complicated subtractions, it may be necessary to take one from lots of columns, but always do it step by step, from left to right.

Note: When adding *and* subtracting in an equation, move from left to right, carrying out the calculations one by one.

2.2 MULTIPLYING WITHOUT A CALCULATOR

"Times" is the same as multiplication; when we times two numbers, it can be referred to as multiplying them together. The product is the result of a multiplication: 3 times 9 is the same as 3 sets of 9, and 3 multiplied by 9. Similar to addition, the order of multiplication does not matter: 3 times 5 is the same as 5 times 3. There are two types of multiplication you should be able to do without a calculator—short and long.

Short multiplication is multiplying (×) by a one-digit number. This can be tricky if multiplying a large number by a one-digit number, so it's best to split the numbers into the groupings: hundreds, tens, and ones, then multiply each individual bit separately (shown in the example below).

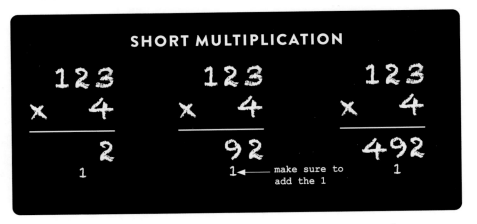

First, write the calculation out with the larger number on top and the smaller number on the bottom, lining up the ones with the ones. Second, multiply the ones digit by the ones digit on top, then the tens digit, then the hundreds digit, one by one. If you get an answer of 10 or more, carry the tens digit of the answer to the next column, as when you're adding.

With long multiplication, you are always multiplying with a two-or-more-digit number. We do the same as for short multiplication, by lining up the numbers on top of each other. For example, when multiplying 123 × 14, separate out the calculation into 123 × 4 first, and then 123 × 10, then add them together in the last step. Remember: if you get an answer of more than 10, then add the tens digit to the next column. In long multiplication, the first answer row will be 123×4, the second row will contain 123×10, and the third will be the sum of both rows one and two. In the second answer row, as multiplying by tens, place a 0 in the ones column.

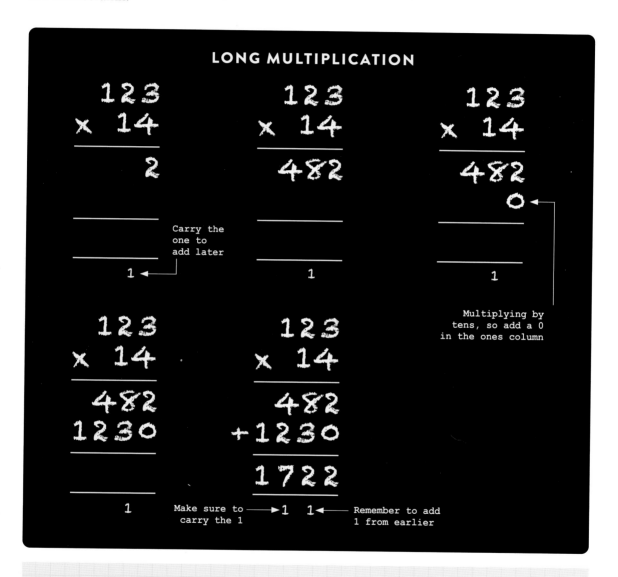

LONG MULTIPLICATION

Carry the one to add later

Multiplying by tens, so add a 0 in the ones column

Make sure to carry the 1

Remember to add 1 from earlier

ANSWER THIS

1. $17 \times 6 =$

2. $252 \times 3 =$

3. $18 \times 12 =$

4. $711 \times 23 =$

2.3

DIVIDING WITHOUT A CALCULATOR

Division is the opposite of multiplication, by seeing how many parts fit into another number. Multiplication results in a larger number whereas division results in a smaller number. As with multiplication, there are two types: short and long division. The order of the numbers is important in division, $20 \div 5 = 4$, which is not the same as $5 \div 20 = 0.25$.

FACT

During the sixteenth century, division such as we learn in schools today was only taught in universities. The method was invented by Henry Briggs, a Professor of Geometry, in 1597, and has remained unchanged to this day. Obviously it's the best way to do it!

Division is about sharing numbers out into parts. For example, if dividing 15 by 3, there are 5 in each part, as $15 \div 3 = 5$. This can be written as 3 goes into 15 five times. Sometimes numbers don't fully divide into another number and there is a little bit left over, this is called the remainder. The remainder can be written as a fraction or with an "r" in front of it.

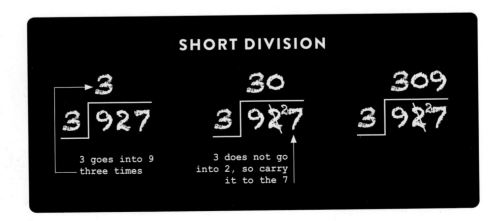

SHORT DIVISION

3 goes into 9 three times

3 does not go into 2, so carry it to the 7

As with multiplication, do each part on its own—for example, divide the hundreds, the tens, then the ones, step by step. It is important to make sure the number you are dividing is in the box, and the number you are dividing by is outside the box—see the sums below.

Long division is used when dividing by a two-digit number (or more). This can look very scary, but you will get better with practice. In our example, we need to find $3456 \div 11$:

First, start with the largest digit, in our case the thousands; 11 does not divide into 3, so we combine the thousands and hundreds digit to get 34. Now, 11 goes into 34 three times with a remainder of 1. Carry this 1 to become 15 in the tens column; 11 goes into 15 once with a remainder of 4. The remainder 4 is carried into the ones column to become 46; 11 goes into 46 four times with a remainder of 5. So the answer is 314 r 5 or $314^5/_{11}$.

LONG DIVISION

2.4 ORDER OF OPERATIONS

Sometimes you will have to do multiple types of calculations, for example an addition and a multiplication in one equation. To know which one to do first, use the standard order of operations, also known as BODMAS, BIDMAS, or PEMDAS, depending on where you are from or how you've been taught. If you do the calculations in the right order, then you will get the right answer.

An operation is just a simple calculation such as adding, subtracting, multiplying, etc. If there are multiple operations in a calculation, it is important to know which one to do first, otherwise you may get the wrong answer. Luckily, there's an easy way to remember what to do first: BODMAS, BIDMAS, or PEMDAS.

BODMAS stands for brackets, other, division, multiplication, addition, and subtraction. In BIDMAS, the "I" stands for indices. In PEMDAS, "P" represents parentheses (another way of saying brackets), and "E" is for exponent (another word for index). What this means is if there are brackets, work them out first, then other things like squaring or cubing, then divide or multiply, then lastly subtract or add.

Multiplication (M) and division (D) are opposites of each other and so are in the same class (both occur before subtraction and addition, and after indices and brackets). Whether you do multiplication or division first depends on the equation, and the equation is always read left to right, so if the multiplication occurs first in the equation, you do that; if the division occurs first, you divide first.

Similarly, as addition and subtraction are opposites, it does not matter if you add or subtract first. Remember: an index, or exponent, is the little number on the top right of a digit that tells us how many times it is multiplied by itself. In the case of 3^4, the ^{4} is the index/exponent, it tells us we multiply 3 by itself four times, so $3 \times 3 \times 3 \times 3 = 81$.

EXAMPLE 1

$$(6 + 8) \times (10 - 2) = 14 \times 8$$
$$= 112$$

This would be different if we ignored the parentheses:

$$6 + 8 \times 10 - 2 = 6 + 80 - 2$$
$$= 84$$

EXAMPLE 2

$$76 - 4^2$$
$$76 - 16 = 60$$

This would be different if we did the subtraction before squaring the number:

$$76 - 4^2$$
$$72^2 = 5{,}184$$

ANSWER THIS

1. Which operation comes first?
a. Subtraction
b. Other/indices
c. Multiplication
d. Brackets/parentheses

2. Work out $16 \times 2 - (1 + 1)$
a. 0
b. 30
c. 32
d. 16

3. Work out $2^2 \times 2 + 2$
a. 8
b. 16
c. 18
d. 10

4. Work out $(10 \times 3) \div 6 + 5$
a. 10
b. 26
c. 36
d. 11

DOING MATH IN YOUR HEAD

Being able to do some simple math in your head, also known as mental math, is very useful in tests and everyday life. So far we have looked at addition, subtraction, multiplication, and division, but each time it was written down. So how do you approach the same sums just by thinking about them?

In order to carry out calculations in your head, it is advisable to try breaking them down into stages. For example, we need to sum the price of a shirt and a pair of pants to get the total price of an outfit for a night out. The shirt costs $102 and the pants $150. First add the hundreds together: 100 + 100 = 200; then the tens: 0 + 50 = 50; finally the ones: 2 + 0 = 2. Lastly, add the three numbers together: 200 + 50 + 2 = $252.

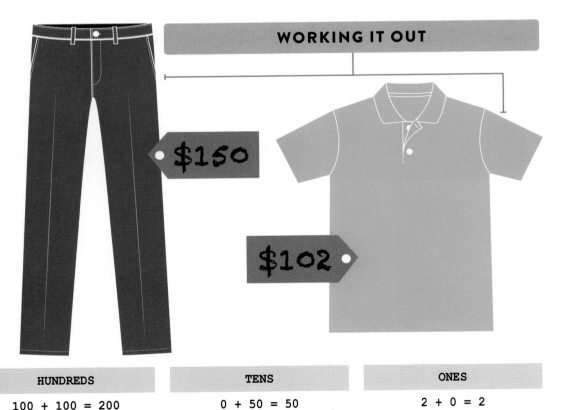

WORKING IT OUT

$150

$102

HUNDREDS	TENS	ONES
100 + 100 = 200	0 + 50 = 50	2 + 0 = 2

Carrying out mental math by breaking it down:

200 + 50 + 2 = 252

Similarly, for subtraction you can break the number down to make it easier. Say we subtracted 23 from 50: we could break the 23 into 20 and 3. So the calculation can be done in two stages: $50 - 20 = 30$; $30 - 3 = 27$.

Sometimes it's easier to make the simpler calculation first that takes us to the nearest ten, hundred, or thousand, then add the remaining. If we are adding 60 to 355, we can break the 60 down. If we add 45 to 355 we get to 400, and then have 15 left over to add, so it is 415.

Lastly, if the number we are using is near 10, we can make the calculation easier by using 10, then accounting for the difference. If we wanted to calculate $38 - 9$ in our head, we could use 10 first to make $38 - 10$, then add 1. Taking away 9 is the same as taking away 10 and then adding 1. So, the answer becomes $38 - 10 + 1 = 29$.

If multiplying two numbers in your head, it is recommended to break the numbers down into the tens and the ones, and multiply them separately. For example, we want to buy seven pears and they are 54¢ each. How much are they in total? Start by breaking it down into 50×7, then 4×7, and adding them together (see right):

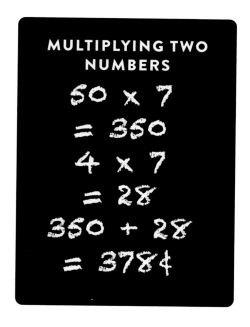

MULTIPLYING TWO NUMBERS

50×7

$= 350$

4×7

$= 28$

$350 + 28$

$= 378¢$

ANSWER THIS

Without writing out any calculations, try to answer the following:

1. $220 + 15 =$

2. $341 + 29 =$

3. $380 - 16 =$

4. $732 - 211 =$

5. $64 \times 9 =$

2.6

MULTIPLYING BY 10s, 100s, 1000s

As we saw in the mental-math pages, when multiplying by large numbers it is helpful to break the number down into tens and ones, then multiply separately. There are a couple of extra tricks when multiplying by 10, 100, or 1000, or even 20, 200, and 2000, that can help speed up the calculations and save you lots of time.

To help with multiplying simple larger numbers, there are three basic rules to follow:

If multiplying a number by 10, move the digits **one** column to the left and fill in with a zero (if needed). Where it is a decimal number, shift the decimal **one** place to the right.

MULTIPLYING BY 10s

$$78 \times 10 = 780$$

When multiplying by 100, move the digits **two** columns to the left and fill in with zeros (if needed). Where there is a decimal number, shift the decimal **two** places to the right.

MULTIPLYING BY 100s

$$23 \times 100 = 2300$$

$$88.91 \times 100 = 8891$$

When multiplying by 1000, move the digits **three** columns to the left and, as always, fill in with zeros. Where there is a decimal number, shift the decimal **three** places to the right.

MULTIPLYING BY 1000s

$$3.4567 \times 1000 = 3456.7$$

The number of places we shift the digits corresponds with the number of zeros in the multiplier: e.g., multiplying by 100, there are two zeros, so we move the digits two columns to the left. The order of the digits doesn't change, just the number of zeros or where the decimal point is placed.

If we have a digit other than one at the beginning of the large number, we can break it down into two stages: first, multiply by the first number, e.g., 2 in 200, then move the digits based on the numbers of zeros.

MULTIPLYING BY 300

$$12 \times 300 = ?$$

First multiply by 3,

$$12 \times 3 = 36$$

then add in the two zeros from 300

$$= 3600$$

ANSWER THIS

1. 13 × 10=
   a. 130
   b. 1.30
   c. 1300
   d. 13

2. 56.937 × 100 =
   a. 5.6937
   b. 0.56937
   c. 569.37
   d. 5,693.7

3. 67 × 1000 =
   a. 670
   b. 6,700
   c. 67,000
   d. 670,000

4. 16 × 40 =
   a. 6,400
   b. 64
   c. 6.40
   d. 640

2.7

DIVIDING BY
10s, 100s, 1000s

Dividing by larger numbers can be daunting, but as with multiplying by 10, 100, 1000, when we divide by those same numbers, we can follow a few simple rules to make it easier. It is important to learn how to quickly divide by 10, 100, etc., as it can make calculations much quicker, in particular when using measurements. It might be easier to remember that dividing by 10s, 100s, or 1000s is the opposite of multiplying by 10s, 100s, or 1000s.

Here are some rules to follow when dividing by 10, 100, or 1000:

When dividing a number by 10, move the digits **one** column to the right and fill in with a zero (if needed). Where it is a decimal number, shift the decimal **one** place to the left.

DIVIDING BY 10s

$$78 \div 10 = 7.8$$

When dividing by 100, move the digits **two** columns to the right and fill in with zeros (if needed). Where there is a decimal number, shift the decimal **two** places to the left.

DIVIDING BY 100s

$$23 \div 100 = 0.23$$

$$88.91 \div 100 = 0.8891$$

When dividing by 1000, move the digits **three** columns to the right and, as always, fill in with zeros. Where there is a decimal number, shift the decimal **three** places to the left.

DIVIDING BY 1000s

$$3456.7 \div 1000 = 3.4567$$

The important thing to notice is that the number of places that the digits are shifted directly relates to the number of zeros in the divider: e.g., dividing by 1000 there are three zeros, so move the digits three columns to the right.

If we have a digit other than 1 at the beginning of the large number, we can break it down into two stages: first, divide by the first number, e.g., 4 in 400; second, move the digits based on the number of zeros. For example, if dividing 12 by 300, divide 12 by the 3, which is 4, then, as there are two zeros, move the digits two places to the right and fill in with zeros: it becomes 0.04.

ANSWER THIS

1. 234 ÷ 10 =
a. 234
b. 23.4
c. 2.34
d. 0.234

2. 870 ÷ 100 =
a. 87,000
b. 87.0
c. 8.70
d. 0.87

3. 69.42 ÷ 1000 =
a. 0.6942
b. 6.942
c. 0.06942
d. 0.006942

4. 16 ÷ 40 =
a. 0.4
b. 2,400
c. 40
d. 0.004

CALCULATING WITH MONEY

One of the most common number calculations you will have to carry out, whether it is mentally or written down, will concern money. Calculations with money are just the same as any other number problems but with currency symbols. It is important to put the decimal point in the correct place, which may mean converting from dollars to cents, for example.

Often we perform calculations with money to see which purchase is the best value for money, or the "best buy." Dexter is attending a basketball game and wants to get a diet soda drink, which comes in sizes small, regular, large, and extra-large. Luckily, the menu sign also tells him that a small is 200 ml and costs $2.00, regular 400 ml at $3.60, large 500 ml at $5.50, and extra-large is 1 liter at $10.50.

To work out the best-value drink, divide the price (in cents) by the weight or volume, in this case ml. First convert all the costs into cents by multiplying them by 100, then convert the 1-liter drink into ml by multiplying by 1000.

MADE SIMPLE
COST PER ML

Trying to determine which drink
is the best value for money by
finding cost per ml

SMALL:
200¢ ÷ 200 ml
= 1¢ per ml

REGULAR:
360¢ ÷ 400 ml
= 0.9¢ per ml

LARGE:
550¢ ÷ 500 ml
= 1.1¢ per ml

EXTRA LARGE: 1050¢
÷ 1000 ml = 1.05¢
per ml

The regular size is the cheapest drink at 0.9¢ per ml.

1. I start out with a $20 bill and I buy dog biscuits worth $13.99 and dog treats at $4.50. How much do I have left over?

2. For birthday presents, I am given: $50 from my mom, $50 from my dad, $25.50 from my grandma, and my brother gave me all his change, $24.76. How much do I have overall?

3. I'm trying to decide whether to get a small, regular, or large salad. The small salad weighs 100 g and costs $2.50, the medium weighs 200 g and costs $4.20, the large weighs 500 g and costs $10.00. Which salad is a better value for money?
   a. Small salad
   b. Medium salad
   c. Large salad

Say we wanted to buy cans of baked beans; for a pack of 4 it is $3.60, for a pack of 12 it is $9.60. As we are trying to save money, we want to know which one is the better valued pack. To work this out, find the price of one can of beans in each pack by dividing the price by the number of items:

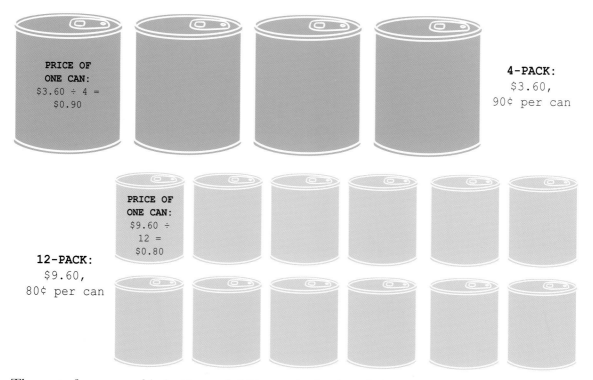

PRICE OF ONE CAN:
$3.60 ÷ 4 = $0.90

4-PACK:
$3.60,
90¢ per can

PRICE OF ONE CAN:
$9.60 ÷ 12 = $0.80

12-PACK:
$9.60,
80¢ per can

The cost of one can of baked beans is 10¢ more in the 4-pack than a can in the 12-pack.

CALCULATIONS

1. 11,743 + 9,074 =
   a. 19,817
   b. 20,817
   c. 21,817
   d. 20,178

2. The difference between 2,328 and 1,176 is:
   a. 1,152
   b. 1,252
   c. 1,125
   d. 1,525

3. Without a calculator find 19 × 7 =

4. Without a calculator find 862 × 12 =

5. Without a calculator find 112 ÷ 4 =

6. Without a calculator find 7294 ÷ 5 =

7. Work out
   7 × 9 + (2 + 8)
   a. 133
   b. 85
   c. 57
   d. 73

8. Calculate
   $(25 + 6) - 8^2 \div 4$
   a. -8
   b. 15
   c. 28
   d. -15

9. Calculate
   486 − 33 in
   your head.

10. Calculate
    28 × 8 in your head.

11. 65.035 × 100 =
    a. 650.35
    b. 6.5035
    c. 6503.5
    d. 6 5035

12. 85 × 200 =
    a. 17,000
    b. 1,700
    c. 170
    d. 170,000

13. 863 ÷ 1000 =
    a. 8.63
    b. 86.3
    c. 8630
    d. 0.863

14. 64 ÷ 80 =
    a. 8
    b. 0.8
    c. 0.08
    d. 0.008

15. Stephanie goes shopping with $50 and spends $27.75 on groceries and $12 on books. How much does she have left over?

16. John is buying some pears: one pear costs $1.05 but a bag of five pears costs $5 exactly. Which one is better value for money?
    a. One pear
    b. Bag of five pears

Answers on page 211

SIMPLE SUMMARY

Calculations are used as a way to figure out a problem. There are four main types: adding, subtracting, multiplying, and dividing.

- The sum of two numbers is found by adding (+) them together.

- Subtraction is the difference of two or more numbers.

- Short multiplication is multiplying by a one-digit number; long multiplication is multiplying with a two-or-more-digit number.

- Division is about sharing numbers out into parts.

- If there are multiple operations in a calculation, it is important to know which one to do first using the standard order of operations—BIDMAS, BODMAS, or PEMDAS.

- In order to carry out calculations in your head, it is advisable to try breaking them down into stages.

- When multiplying by large numbers, it is helpful to break the number down into tens and ones, then multiply separately.

- Dividing by 10s, 100s, or 1000s is the opposite of multiplying by 10s, 100s, or 1000s.

- Calculations with money are just the same as any other number problems but with currency symbols. It is important to put the decimal point in the correct place.

3
DECIMALS, FRACTIONS, AND PERCENTAGES

Decimals, fractions, and percentages are different ways of communicating numbers. This chapter will cover how to carry out calculations using decimal and fraction numbers and how to convert between the three different types.

WHAT YOU WILL LEARN

How to write a fraction

Mixed numbers and improper fractions

Comparing fractions

Adding and subtracting fractions

Multiplying and dividing fractions

Percentages

Converting percentages into fractions and decimals

Converting fractions into decimals

INTRODUCTION TO FRACTIONS

Fractions are a way of writing the numbers in between integers (whole numbers). In many calculations we are not just dealing with whole numbers but also parts of whole numbers, and fractions can make that easier. Fractions are also used when something is being divided into equal parts or sections. A fraction will tell you the portion you need, have, or want. The key thing to remember with fractions is that all parts or sections are always equally sized.

Fractions are made up of two parts: the numerator and the denominator. The numerator is the number on the top, and it tells you how many parts you are dealing with. The denominator is the number on the bottom, and it shows you the total possible number of equal parts. If you only have 1 out of 14 equal slices of cake, then you write $^1/_{14}$ of the cake.

Equivalent fractions

Fractions may be equal, or "equivalent," but with a different numerator and denominator. For example, $^1/_4$ is the equivalent to $^4/_{16}$. Being able to adapt a fraction to an equivalent fraction is useful. Imagine you made an apple pie and it was sliced into 12 equal slices. You want to make sure you have ⅓ left for the next day and need to figure out the equivalent

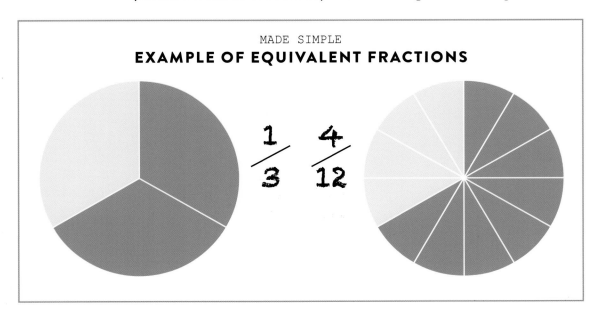

MADE SIMPLE
EXAMPLE OF EQUIVALENT FRACTIONS

fraction out of the 12 slices ($^?/_{12}$). First, you find the number that when multiplied by the first denominator (3) makes the second denominator (12): in this case, it's 4. Then you multiply the original numerator (1) by 4 to get the equivalent fraction: $^4/_{12}$. This means you need to leave 4 out of 12 slices for tomorrow.

Simplest form

Fractions should be written in their simplest form. To simplify a fraction (i.e., to put it in its simplest form) you have to cancel down. Canceling down involves dividing the numerator and the denominator by the same number. It is very important to use the same integer to divide by, as otherwise it will change the fraction's value. Sometimes you will need to cancel down multiple times, for example $^8/_{12}$ can be canceled down twice before reaching its simplest form of $^2/_3$. Always cancel down fractions as far as they will go.

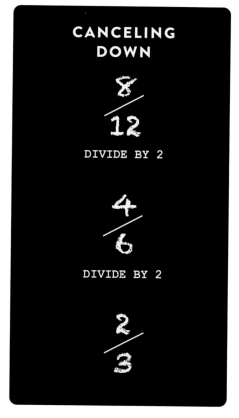

CANCELING DOWN

$\dfrac{8}{12}$

DIVIDE BY 2

$\dfrac{4}{6}$

DIVIDE BY 2

$\dfrac{2}{3}$

ANSWER THIS

1. If I have one slice out of five equal slices of pizza, what is that as a fraction?
   a. $^1/_5$
   b. $^1/_4$
   c. $^5/_1$
   d. $^4/_1$

2. What is the equivalent fraction to $^2/_7$?
   a. $^8/_{21}$
   b. $^5/_{14}$
   c. $^2/_{21}$
   d. $^6/_{21}$

3. Cancel down $^8/_{64}$.
   a. $^2/_{13}$
   b. $^1/_8$
   c. $^4/_{31}$
   d. $^6/_{43}$

4. Write $^{30}/_{75}$ in its simplest form.
   a. $^{10}/_{25}$
   b. $^6/_{15}$
   c. $^2/_6$
   d. $^2/_5$

MIXED NUMBERS AND IMPROPER FRACTIONS

Mixed numbers are a combination of a whole number and a fraction together. For example, $4^2/_5$ is a mixed number, as there are 4 and two fifths. Improper fractions are where the numerator (the number on top of a fraction, remember!) is larger than the denominator. Usually, we do not write numbers as improper fractions, but they can be helpful in calculations.

A mixed number, one that contains a whole number and a fraction together, can also be written as an improper fraction. For example, $^7/_4$ is the same as $1^3/_4$. You can change between the two as improper fractions are useful in calculations, but are not the correct way of writing numbers with fractions.

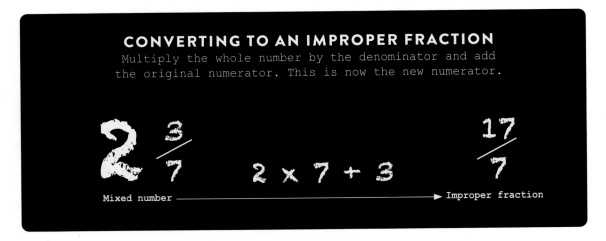

CONVERTING TO AN IMPROPER FRACTION
Multiply the whole number by the denominator and add the original numerator. This is now the new numerator.

$2\frac{3}{7}$ $2 \times 7 + 3$ $\frac{17}{7}$

Mixed number ⸻⟶ Improper fraction

Times tables come in useful here, so make sure you remember them! To convert or change $5^5/_6$ into an improper fraction, first, take the whole number and multiply that by the denominator: $5 \times 6 = 30$. Second, add that value to the numerator: $30 + 5 = 35$. Last, place that value on top of the original denominator: $^{35}/_6$.

FACT

In a proper fraction, the numerator is always smaller than the denominator. If the numerator is the same or larger, it becomes an improper fraction and it must be converted to and written as a mixed number for the final answer.

Changing an improper fraction into a mixed number seems to be trickier for some people, but you can do it in a few simple steps. Let's convert $^{41}/_7$. The first step is to see how many times the denominator goes into the numerator fully: 7 goes into 41 five times fully, as in $7 \times 5 = 35$, therefore 5 is the whole number.

The second step is to see how much is left of the original numerator, and that becomes the new numerator: 35 is accounted for by the whole number, we have 6 left $(41 - 35 = 6)$. This 6 becomes the new numerator and so our fraction portion is $^6/_7$. Now put it all together: the whole number + the fraction = $5^6/_7$.

CONVERTING TO A MIXED NUMBER

See how many times the denominator goes into the numerator. This is now the whole number, and whatever is left is the new numerator.

$$\frac{23}{9}$$

$$9 \times 2 = 18$$
$$23 - 18 = 5$$

Improper fraction ⟶ Mixed number

3.3 COMPARING FRACTIONS

Sometimes we need to compare two amounts that happen to be fractions to see which is larger or smaller. When two fractions have the same denominator, we can easily see which one is bigger or smaller by looking at the numerator—in this case, the bigger the numerator, the larger the number. However, when we compare fractions with different denominators, we have to perform a couple of calculations before we can even compare them.

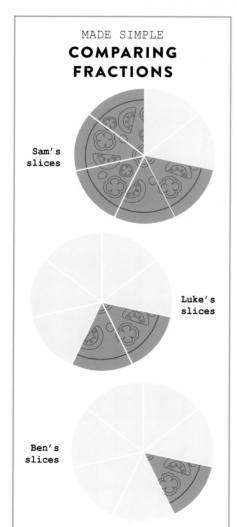

MADE SIMPLE
COMPARING FRACTIONS

Sam's slices

Luke's slices

Ben's slices

When the denominators of the fractions we want to compare are the same, we merely look at the numerator: if the numerator is the biggest number, that fraction is the biggest.

For example, Sam, Luke, and Ben each had a pizza cut into seven slices. They ate the following fractions respectively: $\frac{2}{7}$, $\frac{5}{7}$, $\frac{6}{7}$. Who ate the most of their pizza? As the denominator is the same, we do not need to do anything other than look at the numerator, and the largest number is 6, so that fraction is the biggest; therefore, Ben ate the most.

If the denominators of the two fractions are different, before we can compare them, we must make the denominator the same, thus making two equivalent fractions that can be easily compared. To make the denominator the same, find a common multiple—a number in both the denominators' times tables. Remember: Whatever number you multiply the denominator by, you must multiply the numerator by as well, to keep it an equivalent fraction.

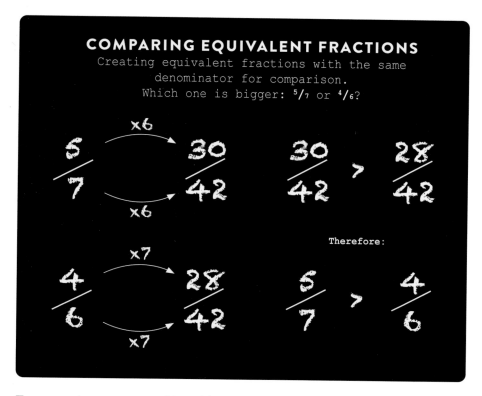

COMPARING EQUIVALENT FRACTIONS

Creating equivalent fractions with the same denominator for comparison.
Which one is bigger: $^5/_7$ or $^4/_6$?

For example, to compare $^5/_7$ and $^4/_6$, identify a multiple of both 7 and 6 (the denominators): 42 is in both the six and seven times tables. Next, turn the fractions into equivalent fractions with 42 as the denominator: $^{30}/_{42}$ and $^{28}/_{42}$.

Now that the denominators are the same, compare the numerators and see that 30 is greater than 28, therefore this fraction is bigger. If one of the numbers is a mixed number, first turn it into an improper fraction before changing the denominator.

ANSWER THIS

1. Which fraction is smallest?
$^9/_{15}$, $^3/_{15}$, $^2/_{15}$, $^{14}/_{15}$

2. Put $^1/_2$, $^2/_3$, $^2/_6$, and $^2/_5$ in order, starting with the smallest.

3. Which two fractions are equivalent?
$^6/_{10}$, $^5/_9$, $^{36}/_{50}$, $^4/_{17}$, $^8/_{36}$, $^{30}/_{54}$

4. Put $1^1/_2$, $1^3/_7$, and $1^5/_{11}$ in order, from large to small.

LESSON 3.4

ADDING AND SUBTRACTING FRACTIONS

We have learned how to write fractions, convert them, find equivalents, and test which is biggest or smallest. However, we have yet to use them in a calculation. Adding and subtracting with fractions looks complicated but it really isn't, although it does often require one or two extra steps.

FACT

To find a common denominator for a group of fractions, first find the lowest multiple common to all the denominators. If the lowest one is not obvious, multiply the two denominators together to create a new denominator. Cancel down at the end.

When adding or subtracting fractions, they all have to have the same denominator. Similarly to the previous section of comparing fractions (see page 56), we often need to convert the denominator thereby creating equivalent fractions. Once we have equivalent fractions with the same denominator, we then just add or subtract the numerators as needed and the denominator stays the same. To calculate:

$$\frac{1}{3} + \frac{4}{5} - \frac{2}{4}$$

First, find the lowest common denominator: the lowest common multiple of 3, 4, and 5 is 60. Second, write the equivalent fractions, as below.

$$\frac{1}{3} = \frac{20}{60} \quad \frac{4}{5} = \frac{48}{60} \quad \frac{2}{4} = \frac{30}{60}$$

The calculation then becomes:

$$\frac{20}{60} + \frac{48}{60} - \frac{30}{60} = \frac{38}{60} = \frac{19}{30}$$

(notice canceling down from ³⁸/₆₀).

Adding and subtracting fractions can become quite complicated when using mixed numbers (remember: they are whole numbers and fractions). You must turn them into improper fractions, change the denominators as necessary, then add or subtract the numerators as usual. For example, to do the following calculation:

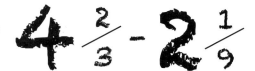

First, make the fractions into improper fractions (go back to the previous section if you can't remember how to do this):

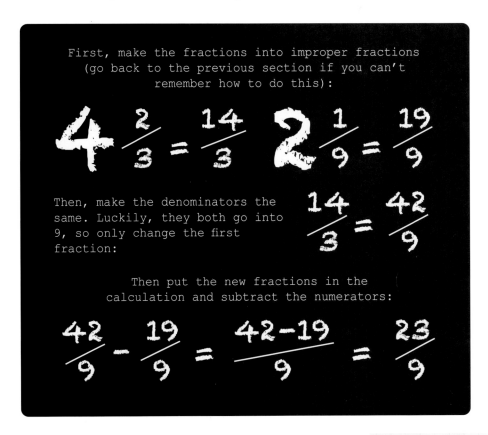

Then, make the denominators the same. Luckily, they both go into 9, so only change the first fraction:

$$\frac{14}{3} = \frac{42}{9}$$

Then put the new fractions in the calculation and subtract the numerators:

$$\frac{42}{9} - \frac{19}{9} = \frac{42-19}{9} = \frac{23}{9}$$

In the example above:

When adding or subtracting with mixed numbers, you will often find the answer is an improper fraction, so you must remember to convert it back to a mixed number. In our example:

$^{23}/_9 = 2^5/_9.$

ANSWER THIS

1. $^3/_4 + {}^1/_6 =$

2. $^{11}/_{15} - {}^1/_3 =$

3. $1^2/_7 + {}^3/_4 - {}^3/_8 =$

4. $4^5/_{12} - 1^3/_8 + 2^8/_9 =$

MULTIPLYING AND DIVIDING FRACTIONS

When adding and subtracting fractions, the denominator must be the same; however, this is not necessary when multiplying or dividing with fractions. In multiplication of fractions, you just multiply the top by the top, and the bottom by the bottom. When dividing fractions, you flip the second fraction then multiply the two fractions. If you have a mixed number, turn it into an improper fraction first, then carry out the calculation.

To multiply by a whole number, you just multiply the numerator (the top number) by the whole number. The denominator does not change. For example, Linus is baking some mini cakes for his friends. He knows that everyone will eat around ¼ of a mini cake, and he has 11 friends coming over. To find out how many cakes he needs to make, he multiplies 11 by ¼ which becomes:

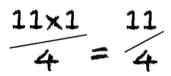

Now convert it to a mixed number:

MADE SIMPLE

MULTIPLYING A FRACTION BY A WHOLE NUMBER

Only multiply the numerator; the denominator stays the same.

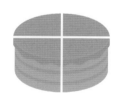

So now we know Linus's friends will eat almost three mini cakes.

When multiplying one fraction by another fraction, you just multiply the numerator by the numerator and then the denominator by the denominator (or simply the top by the top and then the bottom by the bottom). For example, we want to calculate two fifths multiplied by three fourths:

$$\frac{2}{5} \times \frac{3}{4} = \frac{2\times3}{5\times4} = \frac{6}{20} = \frac{3}{10}$$

When dividing a fraction by a whole number, you just multiply the denominator and keep the numerator the same. To calculate $^3/_7 \div 10$ it becomes:

$$\frac{3}{7\times10} = \frac{3}{70}$$

To divide a fraction by another fraction, there is an additional step: flip the second fraction (the fraction you are dividing by), then treat it like a multiplication by multiplying the numerators and then the denominators. For example, to carry out such a calculation:

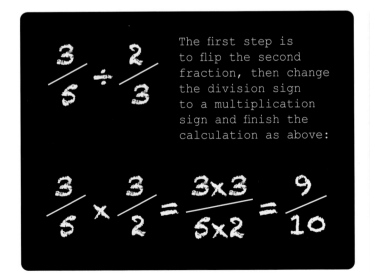

The first step is to flip the second fraction, then change the division sign to a multiplication sign and finish the calculation as above:

$$\frac{3}{5} \times \frac{3}{2} = \frac{3\times3}{5\times2} = \frac{9}{10}$$

ANSWER THIS

Calculate the following:

1. $^2/_9 \times 6 =$

2. $^3/_8 \times ^1/_4 =$

3. $^5/_7 \div 3 =$

4. $^9/_{10} \div ^2/_5 =$

PERCENTAGES: OUT OF 100

Percentages are a way of writing a fraction of 100, or "out of 100." The symbol % is typically used to show percent and that the number is out of 100. For example, 30 out of 100 can be written as 30%. Percentages are used when we are describing a portion or fraction of a total; however, they are also used when talking about more than the total, such as "giving 110%."

Percentages are mostly used to describe a proportion of a total, and this can be calculated with or without a calculator. If the total number is a factor or multiple of 100, then it can be done relatively easily without a calculator by making an equivalent fraction.

CALCULATING PERCENTAGE
Use the formula:

$$\frac{Portion}{Total} \times 100 = Percentage$$

For example: 26 out of 50 apples were eaten, the rest were left. What percentage of apples were eaten that day? First convert it to a fraction by putting the number of apples eaten as the numerator over the total number of apples as the denominator, so it becomes ²⁶/₅₀. As a percentage is out of 100, we can find the equivalent fraction where 100 is the denominator. To get from 50 to 100, multiply by two, therefore multiply the numerator by two as well:

$$\frac{26}{50} = \frac{52}{100}$$

Therefore, it is 52 out of 100, or 52%.

Sometimes, the fractions are not so easily converted, and a calculator is necessary. For example, 13 friends took a trip to the beach for the day. Only four remembered to bring towels. What percentage of the group brought towels? The method above without a calculator won't work, so we have to use a calculator. First, write it out as a fraction: the numerator is the number of people with a towel (4) and the denominator is the total number of people (13): $^4/_{13}$. You can either put it straight into your calculator as a fraction, or type $4 \div 13$, and press equals. This will give you a decimal number; to convert it into a percentage just multiply by 100. In our example this is $0.3076\ldots \times 100 = 30.76\%$. You may be required to round the number to the nearest one, which would be 31%.

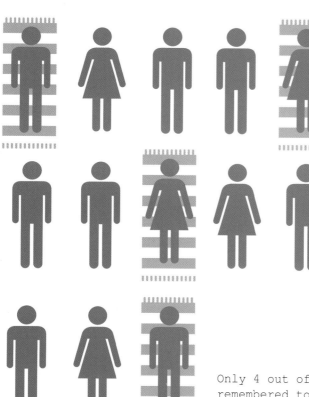

ANSWER THIS

Convert the following into percentages; if necessary, round to the nearest whole number:

1. 5 out of 20

2. 3 out of 25

3. 16 out of 19

4. 23 out of 36

Only 4 out of 13 people remembered to bring towels, which means that approximately 31% of people have towels.

3.7 CONVERTING PERCENTAGES INTO FRACTIONS AND DECIMALS

It is easier to use percentages in a calculation by converting the figure to either a decimal or a fraction. Converting into a fraction is easy when you remember that a percentage is just a number out of 100; therefore, the numerator is the percentage, and the denominator is 100. To convert a percentage into a decimal number, divide by 100.

When converting percentages into fractions, the first step is simple: put the percentage as the numerator, then 100 as the denominator. Always cancel down the fraction to its simplest form. For example, 34% converted into a fraction is $^{34}/_{100}$; canceled down, it becomes $^{17}/_{50}$. This last step, canceling down, can be a little tricky, so make sure you know your times tables to make it quicker. In addition, there are a few common percentages and fractions equivalents that come up often, so it is worth trying to learn these by heart.

To convert a percentage to a decimal, divide the percentage by 100: 86% = 86 ÷ 100 = 0.86. Remember that when you divide by 100 there are two 0s, so shift the decimal two places to the left, or shift the numbers two places to the right, filling in with zeros if needed (see page 44).

PERCENTAGES TO DECIMALS TO FRACTIONS

Percentage (%)	Decimal	Fraction
10	0.1	$^{1}/_{10}$
20	0.2	$^{1}/_{5}$
25	0.25	$^{1}/_{4}$
33.3	0.333	$^{1}/_{3}$
50	0.5	$^{1}/_{2}$
75	0.75	$^{3}/_{4}$
80	0.8	$^{4}/_{5}$
100	1.0	$^{1}/_{1}$

Converting from percentages to decimals should become second nature with a bit of practice. To go from decimals to percentages, multiply by 100, so shift the decimal two places to the right. For example, 0.68 as a percentage is 68%.

PERCENTAGES IN SALES

10% off
$75...

SALE
10%
DISCOUNT!

$75

Percentages are often used in sales, so understanding how to calculate simple percentages in your head can be very useful.

10% of $75 = $7.50
NEW COST $67.50

ANSWER THIS

Without writing out any calculations, try to answer the following:

1. Convert 23% to a fraction.

2. Convert 55% to a fraction.

3. Convert 39% to a decimal.

4. Convert 0.98 to a percentage.

3.8 CONVERTING FRACTIONS INTO DECIMALS

Depending on the calculations or the circumstances, you may need to convert fractions into decimal numbers and vice versa. Fractions are a way of writing the numerator divided by the denominator; the line in between means divide by: $\frac{1}{5} = 1 \div 5$. If you have a calculator, you can just divide the numerator by the denominator. However, sometimes there's no way around having to learn how to do it by hand.

FACT

If you take a close look at the division sign, it looks like a fraction with dots where the numbers are supposed to be. This should help you remember that fractions are just another way of writing a division calculation.

When converting fractions to decimals, take a close look at the denominator: if it is a factor of 10, 100, or 1000, you may be able to convert it quickly to an equivalent fraction and then a decimal. In other cases, you will have to carry out the division either by hand or with a calculator. For example, to convert $\frac{2}{5}$ into a decimal number, first look at the denominator—it is a factor of 10. You can then convert it to something over 10: $\frac{4}{10}$ which becomes $4 \div 10 = 0.4$. This method is very quick if you can remember the rules for dividing by 10, 100, or 1000 (see page 44).

However, the denominator is not always a factor of 10, 100, etc., and so it's necessary to carry out a division. For example, to find out $\frac{5}{16}$ as a decimal number, remember that another way of writing it is $5 \div 16$, so draw out the division as shown in the illustration to the right. You would write 5 as 5.0000, so if there are any tenths, hundredths, thousandths, etc. in the answer you can calculate them. As 5 does not divide by 16, write a 0 on top of the ones column and carry the 5 to the tenths column; 16 goes into 50 three times, with 2 left over, so write 3 in the tenths column on the top and carry the 2, and so on. This leaves us with the answer of 0.3125.

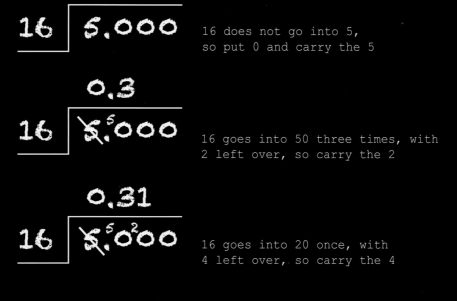

CONVERT ⁵⁄₁₆ INTO A DECIMAL

Division by hand to convert a fraction into a decimal number:

16 ⟌ 5.000 — 16 does not go into 5, so put 0 and carry the 5

0.3
16 ⟌ 5.000 — 16 goes into 50 three times, with 2 left over, so carry the 2

0.31
16 ⟌ 5.000 — 16 goes into 20 once, with 4 left over, so carry the 4

0.312
16 ⟌ 5.000 — 16 goes into 40 twice, with 8 left over. Keep going until you have three or four decimal numbers.

If you still have a remainder at the fifth decimal place, finish the calculation and round up to the fourth decimal place, as otherwise you could go on forever!

ANSWER THIS

Convert the following fractions to decimals
(where necessary, round to the nearest thousandth):

1. ³/₁₀₀

2. ¹³/₂₀

3. ³/₈

4. ⁴/₉

DECIMALS, FRACTIONS, AND PERCENTAGES

1. **A pie is cut into eight equal slices and three are eaten. What fraction of the cake has been eaten?**

   a. $^3/_8$

   b. $^1/_8$

   c. $^3/_5$

   d. $^5/_8$

2. **Write $^{24}/_{80}$ in its simplest form.**

   a. $^3/_{20}$

   b. $^3/_{10}$

   c. $^{12}/_{40}$

   d. $^6/_{20}$

3. **Convert $4^3/_{11}$ into an improper fraction.**

4. **Change $^{53}/_7$ into a mixed number.**

5. **Which fraction is the smallest?**

   a. $^1/_{13}$

   b. $^{12}/_{13}$

   c. $^4/_{13}$

   d. $^9/_{13}$

6. **Put $2^2/_5$, $2^5/_9$, and $2^1/_6$ in order, starting with the smallest.**

7. **$1^7/_9 + 2^1/_{11} =$**

8. **$4^4/_5 + 3^2/_3 - ^1/_4 =$**

9. **Calculate $^4/_9 \times ^3/_7 =$**

10. **Calculate $^7/_{11} \div ^3/_4 =$**

11. **Write 4 out of 40 as a percentage.**

    a. 20%

    b. 4%

    c. 10%

    d. 40%

12. **Write 27 out of 49 as a percentage, rounded to the nearest whole number.**

    a. 49%

    b. 48%

    c. 27%

    d. 55%

13. **Convert 64% to a fraction.**

14. **Convert 37% to a decimal.**

15. **Convert $^{13}/_{100}$ into a decimal number.**

16. **Convert $^5/_{23}$ into a decimal number, rounded to the nearest hundredth.**

Answers on page 212

SIMPLE SUMMARY

Decimals, fractions, and percentages are different ways of communicating numbers. They can be used in calculations and you can convert between the three different types.

- Fractions are a way of writing the numbers in between integers, and consist of the numerator and the denominator.

- All parts or sections of fractions are always equally sized.

- Mixed numbers are a combination of a whole number and a fraction.

- When two fractions have the same denominator, the bigger the numerator, the larger the number.

- If the denominators of two fractions are different, make the denominator the same in order to compare.

- When adding or subtracting fractions, they should all have the same denominator.

- In multiplication of fractions, multiply the top by the top, and the bottom by the bottom.

- When dividing fractions, flip the second fraction then multiply the two fractions.

- Percentages are a way of writing a fraction of 100, or "out of 100."

- To convert a percentage into a fraction, the numerator is the percentage, and the denominator is 100; to convert a percentage into a decimal number, divide by 100.

4

MEASUREMENTS: HOW AND WHY WE MEASURE THINGS

Measurement is the assignment of a number to something that tells us its size or amount. Common measurement units are useful for comparing between the sizes or amounts of things—the different types of standard units and measurement systems are covered in this section. Additionally, you will discover how to convert units both within a measurement system and between the different systems.

WHAT YOU WILL LEARN

What is time?

Units of measurement

Imperial and metric units

Converting units

Perimeters

Calculating and estimating areas

Calculating volumes

4.1 WHAT IS TIME?

Time is used to describe or measure the duration of an event. There are standardized or set measurements for time, from the smallest amount, e.g., a second, up to large amounts, e.g., millennia. Even though it is standardized, in that a minute is 60 seconds, time can be felt differently depending on the activity at hand.

The way we measure time is in seconds, minutes, hours, days, weeks, months, years, decades, millennia, etc. Most of the measures stay the same; however, a month can be 28–31 days long and a year can be 365 or 366 days (for a leap year) long. Key things to remember are there are 7 days in a week; 12 months in a year; 24 hours in a day; 60 minutes in an hour; and 60 seconds in a minute. These standardized measures stemmed from the Babylonians in approximately 2000 BC and haven't been changed since.

Different types of clocks

In telling the time throughout the day, we either use the 24-hour clock—00:00–23:59, or the 12-hour clock—00:00–11:59 with a.m. or p.m. For the morning hours, between midnight and noon, a.m. is used; from noon to midnight, p.m. is used. Timetables and schedules can be written in either—there is not a standard format—so it is important to understand both.

Converting from a 12-hour clock to a 24-hour clock is relatively simple: if the time is in the a.m., then leave the number as is; if the time is in the p.m., then add 12 to the hour number. To convert from the 24-hour clock back to a 12-hour clock, minus 12 from the number only if the original number is greater than 12. If the original number is greater than 12, we write p.m. after it; if the original number is less than 12, then we use a.m.

USING THE SUN

Sundials show different times of day depending on the shadow.

Calculating using time

Quite often we have to carry out a calculation using times, for example, figuring out when a movie will finish. When using times in calculations, it is best doing it in stages. For example, we are going to see the new superhero movie and it starts at 7:05 p.m., or 19:05, and lasts 2 hours and 50 minutes. When will it finish (assuming the cinema doesn't show 30 minutes of trailers)? The simplest way to find out is to add the hours first, so it becomes 7:05 + 2:00, which makes it 9:05. Then we add the minutes to the minutes section: 9:05 + 0:50—therefore, the film ends at 9:55 p.m.

MADE SIMPLE

CONVERTING TIME

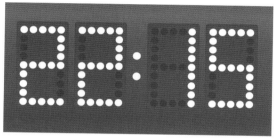

Normal 12-hour analog clock showing 6:40, and we know it is 6:40 p.m., so add 12 to 6 to make it 18:40.

Digital 24-hour clock showing 22:15, so minus 12 from this and it is 10:15. We know it is 10:15 p.m., as the original number was greater than 12.

ANSWER THIS

1. What is 19:40 when converted to the 12-hour clock?

2. Convert 11:55 p.m. to the 24-hour clock.

3. How many minutes in a week?
   a. 1,440
   b. 11,520
   c. 10,080
   d. 8,640

UNITS OF MEASUREMENT

When talking about measurements, it is important to use units as they tell us what a number is referring to, for example, 16 feet means 16 lots of 1 foot. Standard units are consistent, regardless of who is doing the measuring. Units currently in use as standard units of measurements include imperial units, metric units, and the International System of Units (SI).

To measure standard units, you must use the appropriate equipment. Luckily, there are readily available tools used for measuring. For measuring lengths, use a ruler with inch and centimeter marks, or a longer tape measure with foot and meter marks as well. Scales measure weights such as pounds, kilograms, ounces, and grams. Measuring cups are used to measure volumes of liquids in fluid ounces and pints, or milliliters and liters. Stopwatches are used to accurately record time in seconds, minutes, hours, etc. It is important to use the most appropriate unit for the circumstances. The weight of a blue whale is between 100 and 150 tons, which is the equivalent of 200,000– 300,000 pounds. In this instance, tons are a more appropriate measure to use. A field mouse, on the other hand, weighs approximately 0.67 ounces or 19 grams, so tons would not be an appropriate unit in this case.

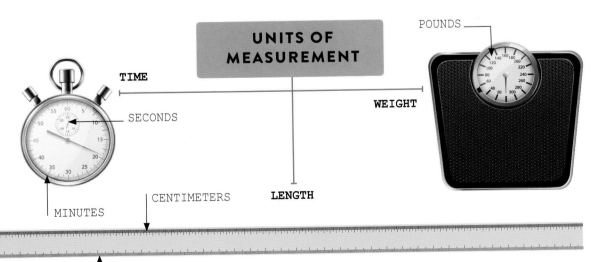

TIME

SECONDS

MINUTES

CENTIMETERS

INCHES

UNITS OF MEASUREMENT

LENGTH

POUNDS

WEIGHT

SELECTING UNITS

It is important to use the most appropriate standard unit for the measurement at hand: you wouldn't use the same weight measurements for a whale and a frog.

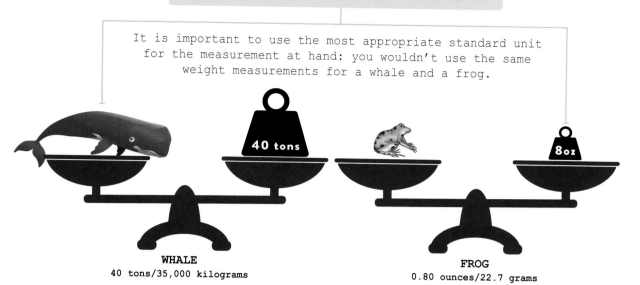

WHALE
40 tons/35,000 kilograms

FROG
0.80 ounces/22.7 grams

Nonstandard units

Units that aren't used regularly or may be different each time, such as shoe, pen, table, or glass, are nonstandard units of measurement. There isn't a standard pen size, for example, as they vary in length. Nonstandard units of measurement may give you a rough idea or decent estimate of size or volume but are not accurate measurements that can be replicated easily.

ANSWER THIS

1. Which standard measurement is used to measure length?
   a. Pounds
   b. Feet
   c. Liters
   d. Minutes

2. Which tool measures weight?
   a. Stopwatch
   b. Scales
   c. Tape measure
   d. Ruler

3. Which of these is an example of a nonstandard unit of measurement?
   a. Meter
   b. Ton
   c. Hair
   d. Inch

4. Which is the most appropriate unit to use for the height of a skyscraper?
   a. Feet
   b. Inches
   c. Pounds

4.3 IMPERIAL UNITS

There are different types of standard units of measurement. The USA predominantly uses the imperial system of measurements, or imperial units. The only other countries to use it predominantly are Liberia and Myanmar. The rest of the world often uses a mixture of imperial and metric measurements or solely metric measurements.

Imperial measures can be used to measure length, area, volume, mass, and speed. Time is not considered either in imperial or metric. Length is measured in inches, feet, yards, and miles. Area is measured in square inches (in^2), square feet (ft^2), and square miles (mi^2). Volume is measured in cubic inches (in^3), cubic feet (ft^3), etc. Mass or weight is measured in ounces (oz), pounds (lbs), stones (st.), tons (not the same as metric tonnes). Lastly, as distance is measured in miles (mi), speed is measured in miles per hour (mi/h or mph).

FACT The imperial system is from the old British Empire. When the USA gained independence from Britain, its government decided to keep the measurement system, despite other countries adopting the metric system.

MADE SIMPLE
CONVERSION FACTORS

LENGTH	1 FOOT =	12 INCHES
	1 YARD =	3 FEET
VOLUME	1 GALLON =	8 PINTS
WEIGHT	1 STONE =	14 POUNDS
	1 POUND =	16 OUNCES

Conversion factors between different imperial units.

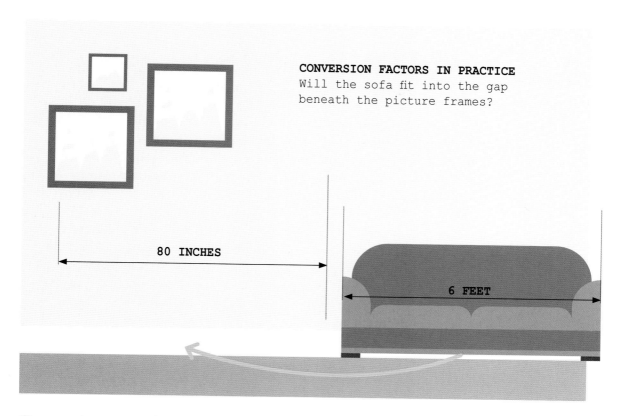

CONVERSION FACTORS IN PRACTICE
Will the sofa fit into the gap
beneath the picture frames?

80 INCHES

6 FEET

Once you have memorized the conversion factors, you will be able to convert between appropriate measurements quickly. Note that if you are going from feet to inches, you would expect the number to be bigger, as 12 is bigger than 1. For example, the sofa is 6 feet long and the space to put it in was measured as 80 inches. To convert the length of the sofa into inches, look at the conversion factors in the table opposite and multiply or divide as appropriate. As there are 12 inches per foot, multiply the number of feet by 12: $6 \times 12 = 72$. The sofa is 72 inches and will fit in the space (phew!).

When going from a smaller measurement to a bigger measurement, the number will get smaller. For example, following a diet and exercise, Deacon the overweight dolphin lost 21 pounds. To convert that to stone, use the conversion table opposite. As there are 14 pounds per stone, divide the number of pounds (21) by 14: $21 \div 14 = 1.5$. Deacon lost 1.5 stones over the summer.

ANSWER THIS

1. How many inches in a foot?

2. How many ounces in a pound?

3. Convert 9 feet into yards.

4. Convert 40 pints into gallons.

5. Convert 12 yards into feet.

4.4 METRIC UNITS

Most countries today use the metric system. It is much easier to use than the imperial system as the units go up in 10s or 100s rather than 12, 14, or 16, for example, in the imperial system. Metric measurements are commonly used in science, technology, engineering, and math (STEM) subjects, or in work produced internationally.

To measure length in the metric system, millimeters (mm), centimeters (cm), meters (m), and kilometers (km) are used. Area is measured in mm^2, cm^2, m^2, and km^2. Volume is measured in mm^3, cm^3, m^3, and km^3. Mass or weight is measured in milligrams (mg), grams (g), kilograms (kg), and tonnes. As distance is measured in km and m, speed is measured in kilometers per hour (km/h or kmph) or meters per hour (m/h).

METRIC

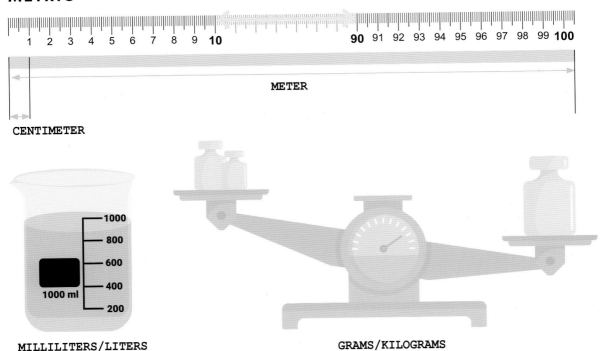

Metric units are widely used in STEM subjects.

The metric system was developed during the French Revolution from 1789 onward. It was in response to the huge variety of measures used in France; the metric system created one universal system that everyone understood.

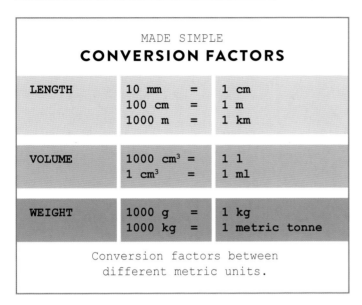

MADE SIMPLE
CONVERSION FACTORS

LENGTH		
10 mm	=	1 cm
100 cm	=	1 m
1000 m	=	1 km

VOLUME		
1000 cm^3	=	1 l
1 cm^3	=	1 ml

WEIGHT		
1000 g	=	1 kg
1000 kg	=	1 metric tonne

Conversion factors between different metric units.

ANSWER THIS

1. How many millimeters in a meter?
   a. 1,000
   b. 1
   c. 10
   d. 100

2. How many kilograms in a metric tonne?
   a. 10
   b. 10,000
   c. 1,000
   d. 1

3. Convert 3.5 m into cm.

4. Convert 1645 m into km.

5. Convert 4.3 kg into g.

Terminology

As you may have noticed, the metric system uses one main stem word and then prefixes. The stem word when measuring length is meter, with the various prefixes of kilo-, centi-, deci-, and milli-. "Kilo" means a thousand, "deci" is one tenth, "centi" is for one hundredth, and "milli" is for one thousandth. By putting one of those words in front of "meter," you are saying what fraction or how many meters. For example, a kilometer is 1,000 meters, a kilogram is 1,000 grams, or a millimeter is one thousandth of a meter.

Converting between different-size units is relatively easy in the metric system, as you are either dividing or multiplying by 10, 100, or 1000, as covered earlier (see pages 42–45). For example, to convert between kilograms and metric tonnes, divide by 1,000 (as there are 1,000 kg per metric tonne).

4.5 CONVERTING UNITS

When numbers have units associated with them, they can only be used in calculations or comparisons if the units are the same. When comparing or calculating different units, the numbers must be converted to the same measurement system and units.

When performing calculations or comparing measurements with many different units, it's vital to convert them all to the same unit before carrying out the calculation. In order to do this, you can use a conversion factor (covered in the previous two sections). Max is 5 ft 2 in. tall and Poppy is 57 in. tall; we want to know who is taller. We can either convert Max's height into inches or Poppy's into feet—as multiplication is always easier than division, let's convert Max's height. There are 12 inches in a foot, so convert the 5 ft first, then add the 2 inches: $(5 \times 12) + 2 = 62$. Max is 62 inches tall and, therefore, is 5 inches taller than Poppy.

FACT

Fahrenheit (°F) is the imperial measure for temperature, and Celsius (°C) is the metric measure. To convert C to F, multiply by 1.8 and add 32. To convert from F to C, minus 32 then divide by 1.8. For example, to convert 37°C to °F, do the following: 37 × 1.8 + 32 = 98.6°F.

MADE SIMPLE
APPROXIMATE (≈) CONVERSIONS

1 inch	≈	2.5 cm
2.2 pounds	≈	1 kg
1 foot	≈	30 cm
1 pint (US)	≈	0.5 liter
1 gallon (US)	≈	3.8 liters
1 mile	≈	1.6 km

Conversion factors between imperial and metric units.

COMPARING LIKE FOR LIKE

To find out who has put more or less gas into her vehicle, convert one of the measures so they are both in the same unit.

Sometimes both imperial and metric units are used. If this is the case, convert all measurements to one system before carrying out the calculation. Tala and Mai put gasoline in their cars: Tala puts in 8 gallons and Mai puts in 34 liters. Who put more gasoline in her car? First, you need to decide which unit system to use: let's use the imperial system here. As Tala's amount is in gallons, we will leave it alone. Mai put 34 liters in her car and there are 3.8 liters per gallon so we divide the number of liters (34) by the conversion factor (3.8): 34 (division sign) 3.8 = 8.95 gallons. Now we can see that Mai put nearly 9 gallons of gas in her car and Tala only put 8 gallons, so Mai put in more.

ANSWER THIS

1. There are two dogs: Alfie and Bertie. Alfie weighs 13 kg and Bertie weighs 32 pounds. Which one weighs more?

2. The tallest redwood tree is 115 m tall and the tallest mountain ash tree is 330 ft tall. Which one is taller?

3. Convert 200°F into Celsius. Round to the nearest whole number.

PERIMETERS: AROUND THE SHAPE

The perimeter is the distance around the outside of a 2-D shape. As it is a length, it is measured in inches, feet, miles, or centimeters, meters, kilometers. The perimeter is the sum of all the sides—the lengths of all the sides added together. The perimeter of a circle is different, however, as it is one length all the way around and has its own formula to calculate it.

To ensure you have counted the whole perimeter, start at a point or corner on the shape and go around the shape systematically, crossing off sides when you have added them. For example, if a triangle has sides with the following lengths: 2 inches, 3 inches, and 4 inches, add them together to get the perimeter: P = 2 + 3 + 4 = 9 inches. Think about how many sides the shape has and make sure you have

MEASURING PERIMETER

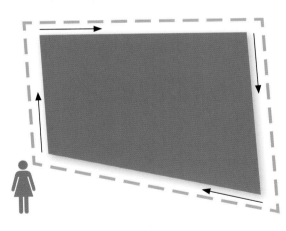

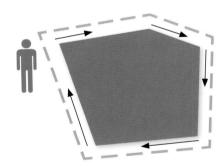

To measure the perimeter of the shape, imagine you are walking around the outside and add up all the lengths along your journey.

FACT

The Chicxulub crater in Mexico was formed when a meteorite hit the earth. It is approximately 110 miles across, which makes the circumference 345.6 miles. If the average person walks 4 miles per hour, it would take just over 86 hours, or 3 days and 14 hours, to walk all the way around the crater.

added that many lengths, e.g., a four-sided shape should have four lengths to add together. Remember, the perimeter is a length and should be measured in inches or feet, or centimeters or meters. If it is a "squared" measurement, it is an area, and a "cubed" measurement is a volume.

Around a circle

The perimeter of a circle is called the circumference—it is the curved edge all the way around the outside. To calculate the circumference, all you need is the diameter of the circle—the straight line passing through the center of the circle from one side to the other—and pi. Pi (π) is a symbol used to represent a particular long number that doesn't change—it is a very long number that starts with 3.14159. Luckily, pi is on most calculators, so you don't need to remember it.

MADE SIMPLE
CALCULATING CIRCUMFERENCE

The largest circle of the Oyu Stone Circles in Japan has a diameter of 46 meters. To calculate the circumference, multiply 46 by π = 144.5 m.

DIAMETER = 46 METERS

CIRCUMFERENCE = Π × DIAMETER

CALCULATING AND ESTIMATING AREAS

The area is how much space a shape occupies, or the surface covered by that shape. If the shape has straight sides, you may be able to use a formula to calculate the area, such as width × length. However, if the shape is uneven with curved lines, a grid and counting squares can be used as an estimation.

Areas are two dimensional, so two dimensions are used to calculate it, and the units are usually squared, e.g., in^2 or m^2. If you see a number with squared units, then you know it refers to area. If a shape has a square grid, then you only have to count the squares it occupies to find its area. In the illustration below, there is a 1-cm grid, therefore each square is 1 cm^2. As we can see, it occupies six squares, therefore it is $6 × 1\ cm^2 = 6\ cm^2$.

USING SQUARES

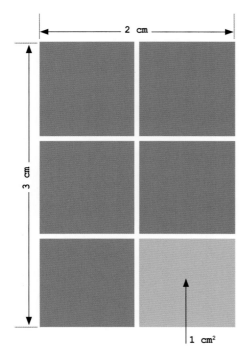

If the shape has a square grid, count the number of squares it occupies to find the area.

The area of a square is quite simple, and we came across it earlier in the section on square numbers (see page 26). As each side is the same in a square, just square the length of one side, e.g., a square with 5-cm sides has an area of $5^2 = 5 × 5 = 25\ cm^2$.

The area of a rectangle is the product of the width multiplied by the length. The area of a triangle is $\frac{1}{2}$ × base of triangle × height of triangle. To find the area of a parallelogram, multiply the base by the perpendicular height (the height at a right angle to the base).

Circle formula

As per usual, circles have their own formulas. To calculate the area of a circle, you need the radius: the distance from the center of the circle to any point on the circumference. The area of a circle = $\pi ×$ radius^2. Remember with BODMAS/BIDMAS/ PEMDAS (see page 38) that indexes or exponents are done first, so be sure to square the radius before multiplying by π. If a circle has a radius of 8 inches, square 8 and multiply by π to get the area: $8 × 8 × \pi = 201.1\ in^2$.

Remember: For the **perimeter, add** the sides to get the total length (one-dimensional measurement); for the **area, multiply** the sides to get the total area (two-dimensional measurement).

MADE SIMPLE
CALCULATING AREA

TRIANGLE	HEIGHT BASE **AREA = ½ × BASE × HEIGHT**
SQUARE	LENGTH **AREA = LENGTH × LENGTH, OR LENGTH^2**
RECTANGLE	WIDTH LENGTH **AREA = LENGTH × WIDTH**
CIRCLE	RADIUS **AREA = Π × RADIUS^2**
PARALLELOGRAM	HEIGHT BASE **AREA = BASE × HEIGHT**

How to calculate area for a triangle, square, rectangle, circle, and parallelogram.

ANSWER THIS

1. Which of the following units is a measure of area?
   a. Square feet
   b. Inches
   c. Miles
   d. Gallons

2. What is the area of a square with sides of 7 inches?

3. Find the area of a triangle with base 8 cm and height 10 cm.

4. If a circle has a radius of 9 feet, what is the area of the circle?

4.8 CALCULATING VOLUMES

The volume of a shape is the amount of 3-D space it takes up—that is, how wide, deep, and tall the shape is. To find the volumes of cubes and cuboids, you find the area of one side then multiply by the depth. As most objects are three dimensional, it is very important you learn how to calculate volumes.

As volume is a three-dimensional measure, the units reflect that, as it is usually described as in^3, ft^3, cm^3, or m^3. If you see one of those units being used, you should immediately recognize it is referring to a volume. Finding the volume of a cube, a 3-D square, is relatively easy, as all the lengths are the same. To find the volume of a cube, cube the length of the side: e.g., a cube with sides of 6 inches long has a volume of 6^3, or $6 \times 6 \times 6 = 216$ cubic inches.

FACT

The Ancient Greek philosopher Archimedes discovered many of the formulas we use today to calculate volumes, such as the volume of a sphere. He famously discovered that when you put an object in the bath, the volume of the water displaced is equal to the volume of the object.

ODD SHAPES

To calculate the volume of an oddly shaped solid you can put it in water.

The difference between the original volume of water and the new volume is equal to the volume of the object.

Original water volume

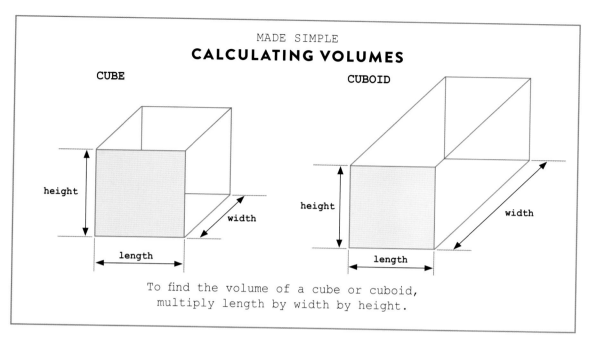

CALCULATING VOLUMES

CUBE

CUBOID

height

width

length

height

width

length

To find the volume of a cube or cuboid,
multiply length by width by height.

The volume of a cuboid (a three-dimensional rectangle) can be found by multiplying the length by the width and the height:

Volume of cuboid =

L × W × H.

In the illustration, the length is 8 inches, the width 2 inches, and the height 5 inches, so the volume is 8 × 2 × 5 = 80 cubic inches.

Circle formula

Like all other measurements involving circles, to find the volume of a ball or sphere you have to use pi (π).

The volume of a sphere =

$^4/_3 \times \pi \times r^3$ (where r = radius).

As an example, the average soccer ball has a radius of approximately 4.5 inches. To calculate the volume, first cube the radius: $4.5^3 = 4.5 \times 4.5 \times 4.5 = 91.125$. Then multiply this by π and then by four thirds: $91.125 \times \pi \times {}^4/_3 = 381.7$ cubic inches. The volume of the soccer ball is 381.7 cubic inches.

ANSWER THIS

1. Calculate the volume of a cube with sides of 9 cm.

2. Find the volume of a cuboid with length 6 inches, width 3 inches, and height 2 inches.

3. Calculate the volume of a sphere with a radius of 3 feet (round to the nearest whole number).

MEASUREMENTS

1. What is 18:45 when converted to the 12-hour clock?

a. 8:45 a.m.

b. 12:45 a.m.

c. 6:45 p.m.

d. 8:45 p.m.

2. How many seconds in a day?

a. 86,400

b. 3,600

c. 100,000

d. 1,440

3. What standard unit is used to measure weight?

a. Meters

b. Pounds

c. Feet

d. Liters

4. Which of the following is an example of a nonstandard unit of measurement?

a. Yard

b. Tonne

c. Inch

d. Toe

5. How many feet in a yard?

a. 12

b. 8

c. 3

d. 16

6. Convert 64 ounces into pounds.

7. Convert 2.78 km into meters.

8. A humpback whale was recorded traveling 7,000 miles, while a great white shark swam for 11,000 km. Which one traveled farther?

a. Whale

b. Shark

9. What is the volume of a cube with a side length of 8 inches?

10. Calculate the perimeter and area of the following shapes:

5 in

a. Perimeter =

Area =

3 cm

9 cm

b. Perimeter =

Area =

4 in   9 in

7 in

c. Perimeter =

Area =

8 m

d. Circumference =

Area =

Answers on page 213

SIMPLE SUMMARY

Measurement is the assignment of a number to something that tells us its size or amount. Common measurement units are useful for comparing between the sizes or amounts of things.

- There are 7 days in a week; 12 months in a year; 24 hours in a day; 60 minutes in an hour; and 60 seconds in a minute.

- In telling the time throughout the day, we either use the 24-hour clock— 00:00–23:59, or the 12-hour clock—00:00–11:59 with a.m. or p.m.

- Units currently in use as standard units of measurements include imperial units, metric units, and the International System of Units (SI).

- The USA predominantly uses the imperial system of measurements.

- Metric measurement units go up in 10s or 100s and are commonly used in STEM subjects, or in work produced internationally.

- When comparing or calculating with different units within the same measurement system, the numbers must be converted to the same units. If the units are from different measurement systems, they must be converted to the same system and then the same unit.

- The perimeter is the distance around the outside of a 2-D shape and is the sum of all the sides.

- Areas are two dimensional, so two dimensions are used to calculate it, and the units are usually squared, e.g., in^2 or m^2.

- As volume is a three-dimensional measure, the units reflect that, and it is usually described as in^3, ft^3, cm^3, or m^3.

5

GEOMETRY: SHAPES, LINES, POINTS, ANGLES

Geometry is the part of math dedicated to the size, shape, dimensions, and angles of objects. In this chapter, you will be introduced to the proper names for 2-D and 3-D shapes, how to identify them, and how to construct them using nets. Furthermore, it covers basic angle rules and bearings.

WHAT YOU WILL LEARN

2-D and 3-D shapes

Shape nets

Measuring and identifying angles

Geometry rules

Lines of symmetry

Angles in parallel lines

Bearings and maps

5.1 2-D SHAPES

A two-dimensional (2-D) shape is a "flat" shape, in that it only has two measurements or dimensions, e.g., length and width. Straight-sided 2-D shapes are referred to as polygons in math. Regular polygons have equal-length sides and angles, for example, a square or an equilateral triangle. Irregular polygons have sides with unequal lengths and the angles are not the same, as those seen in rectangles or scalene triangles.

Quadrilaterals are four-sided shapes—"quad" means four. There are six four-sided shapes you need to be able to recognize: square, rectangle, rhombus, parallelogram, trapezoid, and kite. A square has four equal sides with four right angles, opposite sides are parallel to each other. Where sides or edges are equal they are shown with a dash through them.

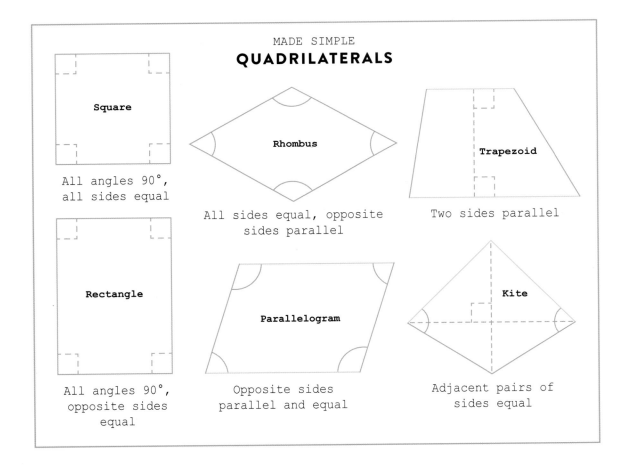

MADE SIMPLE
QUADRILATERALS

Square
All angles 90°, all sides equal

Rhombus
All sides equal, opposite sides parallel

Trapezoid
Two sides parallel

Rectangle
All angles 90°, opposite sides equal

Parallelogram
Opposite sides parallel and equal

Kite
Adjacent pairs of sides equal

A rectangle has two pairs of equal sides and four right angles. A rhombus has four sides of equal length but the angles are not right-angles, so it looks like a slanted square. A parallelogram has two sets of parallel sides, each set is the same length, and the opposite angles are equal to each other—it looks like a slanted rectangle. A trapezoid only has one set of parallel sides; and lastly a kite has two sets of equal-length sides which are next to each other, and there are no parallel lines. The outside edge of the shape is known as the perimeter.

Triangles have three sides, as "tri" means three. There are four types of triangle: equilateral, right-angled, isosceles, and scalene. An equilateral triangle has three equal sides, shown by dashes on the sides, and three equal angles. A right-angled triangle has one 90° angle. An isosceles triangle has two equal sides and two equal angles. Lastly, the sides and angles are all different in a scalene triangle.

Circles are examples of 2-D shapes that lack straight sides. A circle does have two dimensions or measurements, however: the radius and the circumference. The outside edge of the circle is known as the circumference. The distance from the center to the edge of the circle is the radius. The distance across the circle, passing through the center, is the diameter. It is important to remember that the radius is double the length of the diameter.

DIFFERENT TRIANGLES

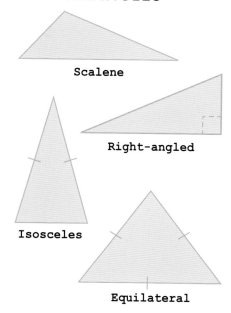

Scalene

Right-angled

Isosceles

Equilateral

CIRCLE

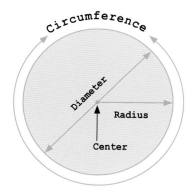

Circumference

Diameter

Radius

Center

ANSWER THIS

1. Draw the following shapes:
a. Rhombus
b. Equilateral triangle
c. Kite
d. Right-angled triangle

2. What is the outside edge of a circle known as?
a. Perimeter
b. Circumference
c. Radius
d. Diameter

5.2 3-D SHAPES

Three-dimensional shapes with flat sides are known as polyhedrons (or sometimes polyhedra). "Poly-" means many, and "-hedron" means faces, so an object with many faces. In regular polyhedrons, each of the faces is the same shape; this shape is a regular polygon, which means they look the same regardless of the side you are looking at. Irregular polyhedrons have different faces, and the faces may even be different shapes, so they may look different from each side.

Polyhedrons have three main identifying features:
1) Vertices (singular vertex), or corners, where three or more sides meet.
2) Faces: sides of the shape.
3) Edges: where two faces meet.

POLYHEDRONS

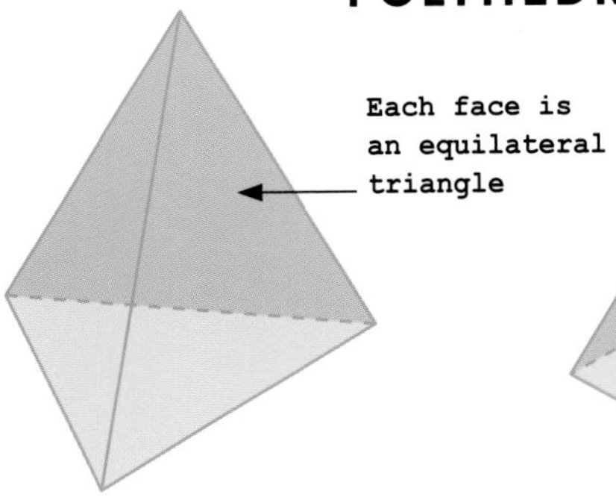

Each face is an equilateral triangle

Face

REGULAR TETRAHEDRON
- 4 faces
- 4 vertices
- 6 edges

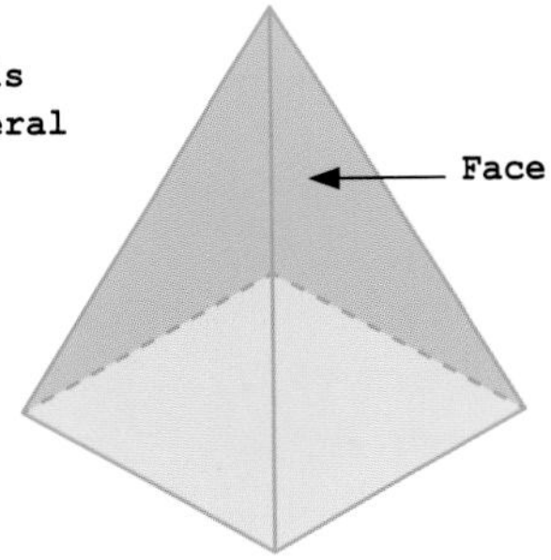

SQUARE-BASED PYRAMID
- 1 square face
- 4 triangular faces
- 5 vertices

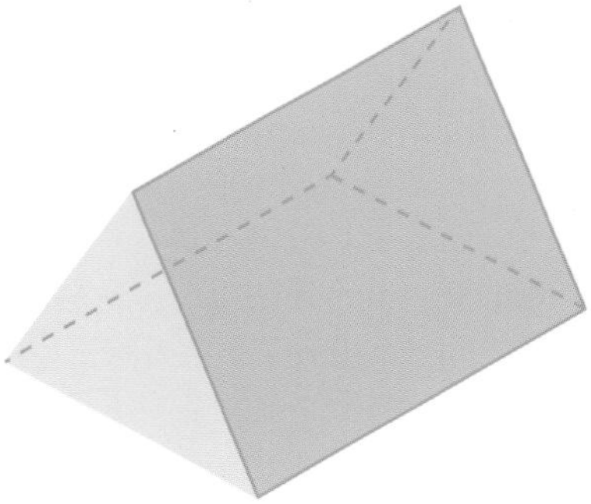

TRIANGULAR PRISM
- 2 triangular faces
- 3 rectangular faces
- 6 vertices

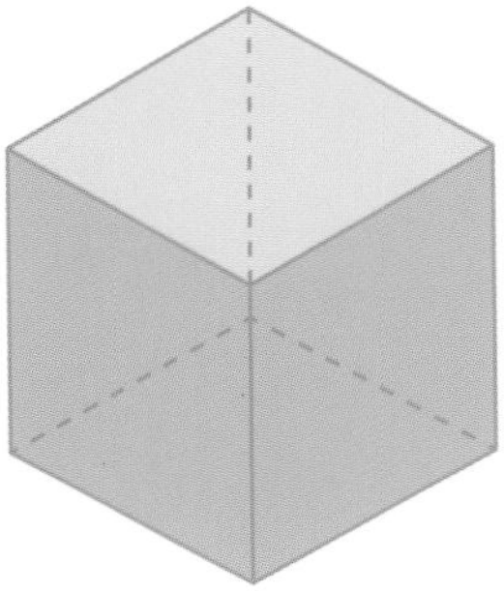

CUBE
- 6 square faces
- 8 vertices
- 12 edges

Vertex (corner)

Edge (where two sides join)

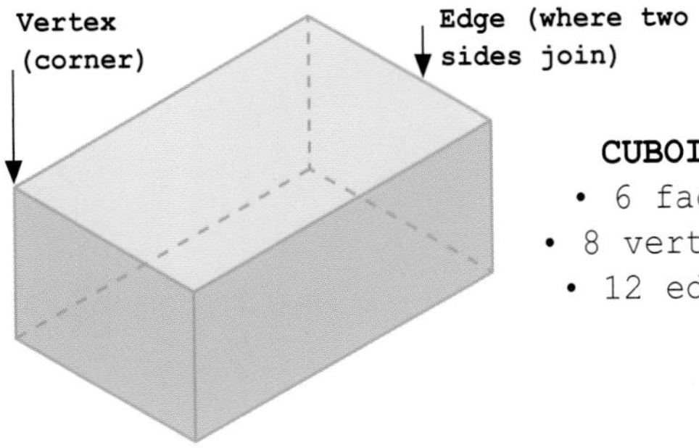

CUBOID
- 6 faces
- 8 vertices
- 12 edges

NON-POLYHEDRONS

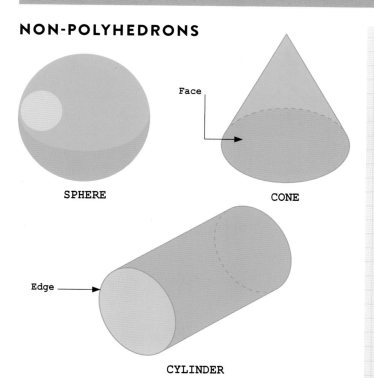

SPHERE

Face

CONE

Edge

CYLINDER

Regular polyhedrons have same-shape sides and look the same no matter which side you are looking at. There are only two regular polyhedrons that you need to know: cubes and regular tetrahedrons.

In irregular polyhedrons, the faces are often different shapes and therefore they won't look the same from each side. You should be able to recognize three irregular polyhedrons: cuboids, triangular prisms, and square-based pyramids.

5.3 SHAPE NETS

Shape nets are shapes that when folded make a 3-D shape. The net of a 3-D shape is what it would look like if it was opened out flat. Quite often there are several nets for one particular shape—there are 11 different net shapes that will fold to make a cube.

It is important to recognize the nets of cubes, cuboids, triangular prisms, cylinders, and square-based prisms as these are likely to be the type of shapes you may need to create, and more complex shapes are made up of these individual shapes added together. Shape nets are useful when calculating surface area of the shape. To find the surface area you calculate the area of each surface and then sum them all together. The descriptions of the faces in the previous section on 3-D shapes may also help with identifying nets if you are unsure. For example, the square-based pyramid has four triangular faces and one square face.

ANSWER THIS

What shape would the following nets make when folded?

1.

2.

3.

4.

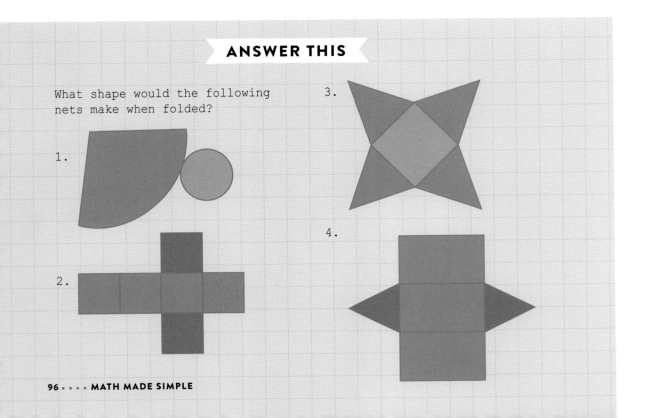

SHAPE NETS FOR COMMON 3-D SHAPES

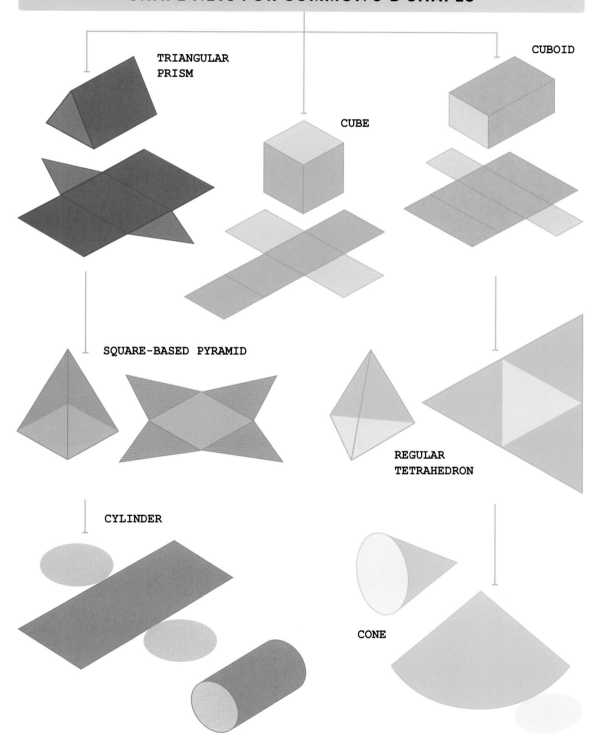

TRIANGULAR PRISM

CUBE

CUBOID

SQUARE-BASED PYRAMID

REGULAR TETRAHEDRON

CYLINDER

CONE

MEASURING AND IDENTIFYING ANGLES

An angle is formed where two lines meet; it is the measure of a turn between these two lines. Angles should always be between 0° and 360°, and the bigger the number, the bigger the turn between the two lines. Angles have different names depending on how big they are: acute, right-angled, obtuse, reflex.

Angles are the amount of turn between two lines; think of it as how far you would have to turn (in a circle on the spot) from facing one line to facing the other. As it is a circle, if you were going clockwise, a quarter turn would be facing to the right, a half turn would be facing behind you, and a full turn would be back where you started.

FACT
Angles are widely used in professions where they have to make something, such as construction or architecture. In order to build chairs or tables, for example, carpenters must be able to accurately measure angles.

MADE SIMPLE
MEASURING ANGLES

TURNS
A quarter 90°, half 180°, and three-quarter 270° turn angle sizes.

PROTRACTOR
Protractors measure angles in degrees. Most protractors are divided into 180 equal parts.

TYPES OF ANGLES AND THEIR NAMES

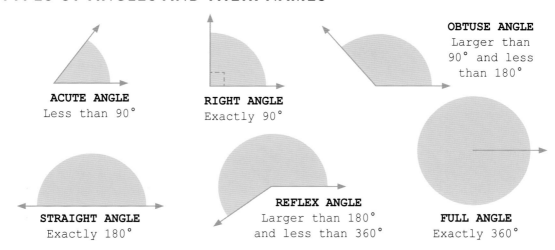

ACUTE ANGLE
Less than 90°

RIGHT ANGLE
Exactly 90°

OBTUSE ANGLE
Larger than 90° and less than 180°

STRAIGHT ANGLE
Exactly 180°

REFLEX ANGLE
Larger than 180° and less than 360°

FULL ANGLE
Exactly 360°

If an angle is less than 90°(or less than a quarter turn around the circle), it is an acute angle. If it is exactly 90° (or a quarter turn), it is a right angle, which is shown by drawing a little square in the angle. If an angle is bigger than 90° but smaller than 180° (bigger than a quarter turn but less than a half turn), it is an obtuse angle. If the angle is larger than 180°, or a half turn, it is called a reflex angle.

Using a protractor
Often you will use a protractor to measure an angle. First, put the cross in the center of the protractor over the corner you want to measure, making sure to line up the bottom line of the protractor with one of the lines from the corner you are measuring. Protractors have two scales, one going left to right and the other going the opposite way. Starting at the bottom line, read off the numbers where the other line (not the one on the bottom) hits the scale (make sure you are starting from 0° on the bottom line).

ANSWER THIS

1. What shape is drawn in a right-angle?
a. Square
b. Triangle
c. Circle
d. Hexagon

2. What name is given to an angle that is greater than 180°?
a. Acute
b. Right-angle
c. Reflex
d. Obtuse

3. When using a protractor, where should you put the cross?

4. An obtuse angle must be bigger than _____ and smaller than_____.

5.5 GEOMETRY RULES

In some cases, angles can be calculated using a set of rules. This may be helpful when the object is not drawn to scale and you need to know the size of the angle. There are set rules for angles on a straight line, around a point, in triangles, and in quadrilaterals. These rules are useful where you need to figure out one angle and have the size of all the others.

Straight line

All angles on a straight line will add up to 180°. For example, with a straight line with one line coming off it, creating two angles, one angle is 102° but we don't know what the other angle is. To work out the unknown angle, minus the known angle from 180. Whatever is left is the missing angle: $180 - 102 = 78$. The missing angle is 78°.

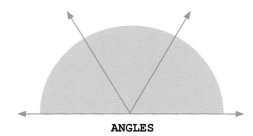

ANGLES
on a straight line

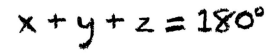

$$x + y + z = 180°$$

Point

Angles around a point add up to 360°. Three lines meet at a point, creating three angles: one angle measures 45°, another angle measures 150°, but the the size of the last angle is unknown. As all angles add up to 360°, using this rule, add the known angles, subtract that from 360, and what's left is the missing angle: $150 + 45 = 195$; $360 - 195 = 165$. The last angle is 165°.

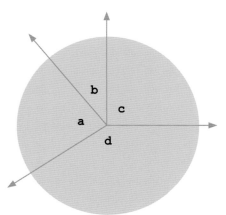

ANGLES
around a point

$$a + b + c + d = 360°$$

Triangles

Angles in a triangle will always add up to 180°. All triangles have three angles, so if you know two of the angles, you will be able to figure out the third by subtracting the other angles by 180—whatever is left is the third angle. For example, for a triangle with angles 36° and 59°, subtract those from 180° to get the final angle: $180 - 36 - 59 = 85°$.

Quadrilaterals

Angles in a quadrilateral will add up to 360°. As all quadrilaterals have four angles, if three angles are known, you can calculate the last one using this rule. For example, a quadrilateral has angles of 88°, 123°, and 96°. As with the examples above, minus these from 360° this time to get the remaining angle: $360 - 88 - 123 - 96 = 53°$.

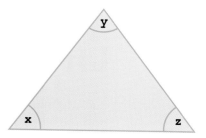

Equilateral

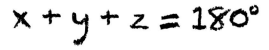

$$x + y + z = 180°$$

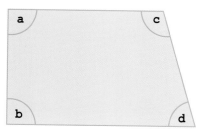

Parallelogram

$$a + b + c + d = 360°$$

FACT Angles stay the same regardless of scale. Imagine a 12 in. and a 24 in. pizza, each cut into 12 slices. The angles at the corners (in the middle) of the pizza would be the same in the 12 in. pizza as the 24 in.

ANSWER THIS

1. All angles around a point add up to:
   a. 100°
   b. 180°
   c. 360°
   d. 90°

2. Two angles in a triangle are each 45°. Find the missing angle.

3. Angles on a straight line add up to:
   a. 360°
   b. 180°
   c. 90°
   d. 10°

4. In a quadrilateral, three angles are 40°, 90°, and 110°. Calculate the missing angle.

5.6 LINES OF SYMMETRY

A shape is considered symmetrical if it is exactly the same on both sides or if it looks exactly the same when turned around. If a central dividing line, known as a mirror line, can be drawn on the shape and is the same on both sides, then the shape is symmetrical. On some shapes, many different lines can be drawn, as the shape may be symmetrical in different directions. Each dividing line is known as a line of symmetry.

 FACT Rotational symmetry is how many times a shape appears the same as it is rotated around. The number of times it is the same is known as order of symmetry.

You may be asked to identify if there are any lines of symmetry and if so how many, so it is best if you are aware of the lines of symmetry in standard shapes (shown in the illustration). It's key to remember that a line of symmetry will divide a shape into two mirror-image halves (mirror-image means they are exactly the same). A square, for example, has four lines of symmetry; these are four different lines that will have the same exact shapes on either side.

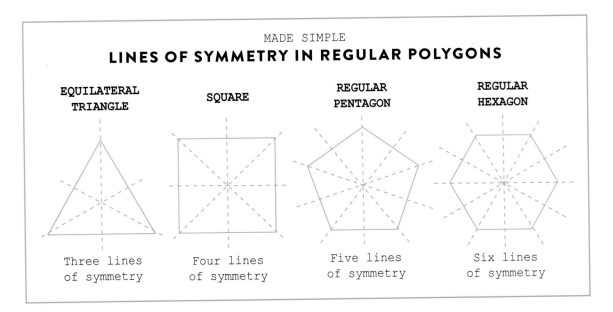

MADE SIMPLE

LINES OF SYMMETRY IN REGULAR POLYGONS

EQUILATERAL TRIANGLE

Three lines of symmetry

SQUARE

Four lines of symmetry

REGULAR PENTAGON

Five lines of symmetry

REGULAR HEXAGON

Six lines of symmetry

LINES OF SYMMETRY IN IRREGULAR POLYGONS

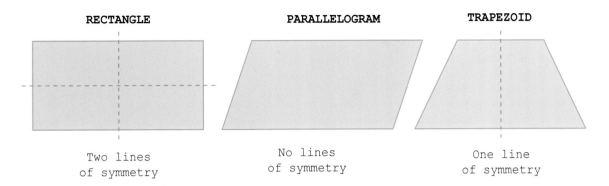

RECTANGLE
Two lines
of symmetry

PARALLELOGRAM
No lines
of symmetry

TRAPEZOID
One line
of symmetry

Regular polygons (shapes with equal-length sides and equal-size angles) will have the same number of lines of symmetry as number of sides. So, a regular octagon will have eight lines of symmetry as it has eight sides.

Be very careful with diagonal lines on quadrilaterals other than squares, as only diagonal lines in squares are lines of symmetry. Rectangles and rhombuses have only two lines of symmetry, parallelograms don't have any lines of symmetry, and trapezoids have one maximum or none at all. One way to check is to try and draw the mirror image that would be produced by your proposed line of symmetry. Another way is to cut out the shape, if possible, and fold it along the symmetry line—if the sides do not match up then it is not a valid line of symmetry. Interestingly, though, as there are an infinite number of lines through the center of a circle, it has an infinite number of lines of symmetry.

ANSWER THIS

1. How many lines of symmetry does a square have?
   a. 1
   b. 2
   c. 4
   d. 8

2. How many lines of symmetry does a circle have?
   a. Infinite
   b. None
   c. 100
   d. 5

3. How many lines of symmetry does a parallelogram have?
   a. 4
   b. None
   c. 1
   d. 2

5.7 ANGLES IN PARALLEL LINES

When a line crosses a set of parallel lines it creates a series of angles. Luckily there are a series of rules to help us figure out the size of these angles. Remember, parallel lines are two or more lines with the same slope and are identified by the same number of arrows on the lines. There are only two different angles formed here and they add up to 180°.

Parallel lines are shown with arrows (pointing in the same direction). When a line bisects, it cuts the parallel lines in two and creates angles. There are three sets of rules to help calculate these angles. Opposite angles are the same. Additionally, as seen in the figures, corresponding angles are the same, as are alternate angles. It's only allied angles that will add to 180°.

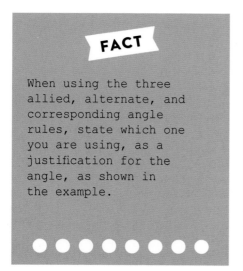

FACT

When using the three allied, alternate, and corresponding angle rules, state which one you are using, as a justification for the angle, as shown in the example.

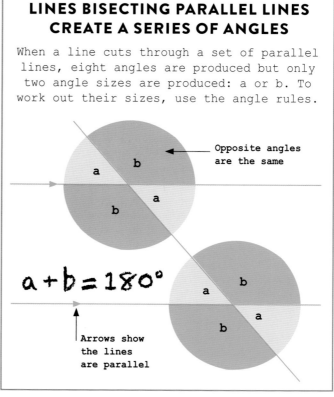

MADE SIMPLE

LINES BISECTING PARALLEL LINES CREATE A SERIES OF ANGLES

When a line cuts through a set of parallel lines, eight angles are produced but only two angle sizes are produced: a or b. To work out their sizes, use the angle rules.

Opposite angles are the same

$$a + b = 180°$$

Arrows show the lines are parallel

Corresponding, alternate, and allied

Angles that are corresponding are always the same size. These are the two angles on the same side as the bisecting line, either both above or both below the parallel lines, and are also known as F-shape angles. Alternate angles are always the same size, and are also known as Z-shape angles. They are found on opposite sides of the bisecting line and within the parallel lines. Allied angles always add up to 180°. They are on the same side of the bisecting line and within the parallel lines. As we saw in the rules section before, if you have one angle, just subtract that from 180 to get the missing angle. Allied angles are known as C-shaped or U-shaped angles.

Three rules for angles in parallel lines

In the drawing below, we can see a set of parallel lines with a line passing through them. One angle is 110° but x and y are unknown. To work out x use the allied rule where these two angles (110 and x) equal 180, this makes x = 70°. As the known angle and the y angle are alternate angles, we know from the rules above they are equal, so y = 110°.

CORRESPONDING ANGLES, OR F-ANGLES

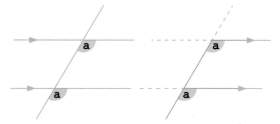

ALTERNATE ANGLES, OR Z-ANGLES

ALLIED ANGLES, OR C-ANGLES

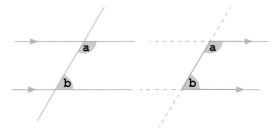

USING THE ANGLES IN
PARALLEL LINES RULES

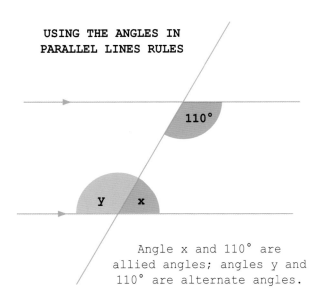

Angle x and 110° are allied angles; angles y and 110° are alternate angles.

BEARINGS AND MAPS

Bearings are angles measured from the North. There are specific rules about how bearings should be measured and expressed. The first rule is that all angles should be measured from the North line. The second rule is that it is always measured clockwise from that line.

Bearings are always measured in the clockwise direction, with North considered to be 000°. They are useful for sailors in particular, as in the ocean every direction may look the same and so sailors needed a method to communicate locations effectively.

North has a bearing of 000°, East is 090°, South is 180°, and West is 270° (note that bearings are always given as three digits). If you can remember these, then it should help you to check your answers and make sure you measure bearings in the clockwise direction. In the drawing, in order to find the angle from the *Mayflower* to the *Jolly Roger* and vice versa, first draw North lines from each ship and a line connecting the two. Place the cross of the protractor on the angle, with 0° on the North line, then measure the angle. The *Jolly Roger* is 040° from the *Mayflower* (always described as "from" rather than "to").

W
270°

▶ ANSWER THIS ◀

1. Should you measure bearings clockwise or anticlockwise from the North line?

2. What bearing is East?
   a. 000°
   b. 090°
   c. 180°
   d. 360°

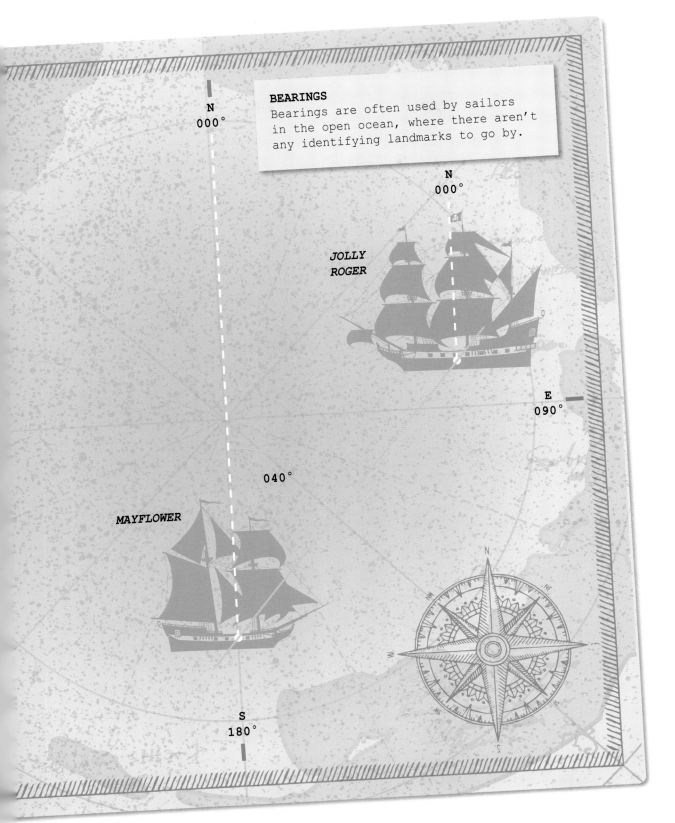

BEARINGS
Bearings are often used by sailors in the open ocean, where there aren't any identifying landmarks to go by.

N
000°

N
000°

JOLLY
ROGER

E
090°

040°

MAYFLOWER

S
180°

GEOMETRY

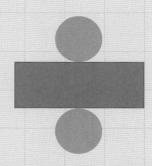

1. How many edges does a square-based pyramid have?

   a. 1

   b. 2

   c. 4

   d. 8

2. How many faces does a cuboid have?

   a. 10

   b. 12

   c. 6

   d. 8

3. In degrees (°), how big is a right-angle?

   a. 90

   b. 180

   c. 270

   d. 360

4. All angles around a point add up to how many degrees?

   a. 0

   b. 90

   c. 180

   d. 360

5. What shape would this net make?

   a. Cube

   b. Cylinder

   c. Cuboid

   d. Pyramid

6. In a triangle where one angle equals 85° and another is 72°, what is the value of the third angle?

   a. 25

   b. 23

   c. 27

   d. 29

7. How many lines of symmetry does a square have?

   a. 4

   b. 2

   c. 1

   d. 0

8. Which shape does not have any lines of symmetry?

   a. Circle

   b. Rectangle

   c. Parallelogram

   d. Regular pentagon

9. What is the rule for allied angles?

   a. They are the same

   b. They add to 180°

10. When using bearings, what direction is 090°?

    a. North

    b. East

    c. South

    d. West

Answers on page 213

SIMPLE SUMMARY

Geometry is the part of math dedicated to the size, shape, dimensions, and angles of objects.

- A two-dimensional (2-D) shape is a "flat" shape, in that it only has two measurements or dimensions, e.g., length and width. Straight-sided 2-D shapes are referred to as polygons.

- Three-dimensional shapes with flat sides are known as polyhedrons, and they have three main identifying features: vertices, faces, and edges.

- The net of a 3-D shape is what it would look like if it was opened out flat.

- An angle is formed where two lines meet; it is the measure of a turn between these two lines and should always be between 0° and 360°.

- All angles on a straight line will add up to 180°; angles around a point add up to 360°; angles in a triangle will always add up to 180°; angles in a quadrilateral will add up to 360°.

- If a mirror line can be drawn on the shape and is the same on both sides, then the shape is symmetrical.

- Opposite angles, corresponding angles, and alternate angles are the same; it's only allied angles that will add to 180°.

- North has a bearing of 000°, East is 090°, South is 180°, and West is 270°.

6

RATE OF CHANGE, RATIO, AND PROPORTION

Rate, ratio, and proportion are all ways to describe how one value relates to another value in some way. Rate of change is how values change over time (for example), ratio is how values relate to each other, and proportion is how values relate to the total. Here you will learn how to write and work with ratios and proportions, and how to calculate rates for three key relationships: pressure–force–area, speed–distance–time, and density–mass–volume.

WHAT YOU WILL LEARN

Ratios

Conversions using ratios

Direct proportion

Compound growth and decay

Pressure, force, area

Percentage change

Maps and scale drawings

Density and speed

RATIOS: COMPARING TWO THINGS

Ratios are a way of describing a relationship between two numbers; they are used to compare two or more things when items are shared unequally or there are an unequal number of objects in multiple groups. For example, if there are 5 goldfish and 2 clownfish in a bowl, the ratio of goldfish to clownfish is 5:2.

When calculating or describing a ratio, it is important to count the total number of objects or items, and then the number of objects of each type. Say there were 12 insects in the garden: 7 are flies and 5 are wasps. The ratio is 7 flies to 5 wasps, or 7:5. The two numbers should add up to the total number of objects, in this case 12.

Ratios can be written as fractions, using the words "for every" or "to," or with a colon. When using the colon, be careful with the order of the numbers; in the goldfish example, if you switched the numbers around to 2:5 it would mean there were 2 goldfish for every 5 clownfish, which is incorrect.

MADE SIMPLE
RATIOS

5 GOLDFISH TO 2 CLOWN FISH = 5:2

FACT

Similarly to fractions, you must always cancel down to simplify ratios. This is done in the same way, by finding a number that can divide into both numbers, e.g., 3:12 can be simplified to 1:4.

Using ratios to solve problems

Sometimes you will need to use a ratio to solve a problem. Let's say that for every trick the dog carries out, it gets 3 treats. How many treats would the dog get if it did 6 tricks? Remember the ratio is 1 trick to 3 treats (1:3), so to get from 1 trick to 6 tricks, we multiply it by 6. You have to do the same to the other side of the ratio, so you multiply 3 by 6, which equals 18.

Ratios can also be used to share out objects. Emily and Edward are sharing a pack of chocolates in the ratio of 3:4. So for every 3 chocolates Emily gets, Edward gets 4. There are 35 chocolates overall and we want to know how many Emily gets. First, we take the sum of the two numbers in the ratio to work out the number of parts: 3 + 4 = 7. Then we divide that total number of chocolates (35) by the number of parts (35 ÷ 7 = 5). This is the number of chocolates per part: 5 chocolates per part—remember the ratio has 7 parts. As Emily has 3 parts of the ratio, times 5 by 3 to get 15. Emily has 15 chocolates and Edward gets 20.

SHARING OUT

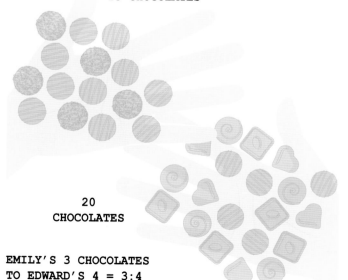

15 CHOCOLATES

20 CHOCOLATES

EMILY'S 3 CHOCOLATES
TO EDWARD'S 4 = 3:4

1. What is the ratio of blue marbles to red if there are 9 blue marbles and 2 red?
    a. 2:9
    b. 7:2
    c. 2:7
    d. 9:2

2. Simplify fully the ratio 12:60.
    a. 1:5
    b. 6:10
    c. 5:1
    d. 4:20

3. On a tree, the ratio of brown to green leaves is 6:5. If there are 60 brown leaves, how many green leaves are there?
    a. 25
    b. 50
    c. 30
    d. 55

4. Finley and Jack order a pizza with 12 slices, Finley has 3 slices and Jack has 9. Find the simplified ratio of Finley's slices to Jack's.
    a. 3:9
    b. 3:12
    c. 4:1
    d. 1:3

6.2 CONVERSIONS USING RATIOS

Ratios can be used to convert measures in proportion to other measures through scaling up or down. This is commonly used in distances and cooking recipes. Ratios tell us the relative proportions of each ingredient, for example, and if we want to increase that ingredient, we need to also increase the other ingredients by the right amount. Remember that we only multiply or divide when converting ratios—never add or subtract—as we are using proportions.

If a recipe has a set number of servings but you want more or fewer, you can use the ratios in the recipe to adapt the amounts. For example, to make 10 pancakes, mix: 1 cup flour, 2 tablespoons sugar, 1 cup milk, 1 large egg.

The ratio of flour: sugar: milk: eggs is 1:2:1:1, for 10 pancakes. One weekend, there is only 1 person and he wants to make just 5 pancakes. Look at the relationship between how many servings the ratio makes and how many are wanted: 10 to 5. Divide 10 by 2 to get 5; therefore, divide all the numbers in the ratio by 2: $^1/_2$:1:$^1/_2$:$^1/_2$, so you need $^1/_2$ cup of flour, 1 tablespoon sugar, etc.

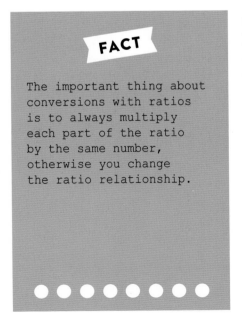

FACT

The important thing about conversions with ratios is to always multiply each part of the ratio by the same number, otherwise you change the ratio relationship.

Scaling up

It is the same to scale up: imagine you want to make 40 pancakes. Again, look at the relationship between the serving number for the original ratio and the number of servings now wanted: 10 and 40. Multiply 10 by 4 to get to 40; therefore, multiply all the numbers in the ratio by 4 to get the correct ratio for making 40 pancakes: 4:8:4:4.

For another example, you have 3 eggs and want to see how much sugar you need to make pancakes using all 3 eggs. The original ratio uses 1 egg, so to get from 1 to 3, multiply by 3. Therefore, multiply the other numbers in the ratio by 3—3:6:3:3. From the new ratio, you need 6 tablespoons of sugar.

MADE SIMPLE
PANCAKES

TO MAKE 10 PANCAKES:

- 1 CUP FLOUR

- 2 TABLESPOONS SUGAR

- 1 CUP MILK

- 1 LARGE EGG

5 PANCAKES
Divide ingredients by 2

10 PANCAKES

40 PANCAKES
Multiply ingredients by 4

When scaling recipes up or down, increase or decrease amounts in proportion with the other ingredients, based on their ratios.

ANSWER THIS

1. The height to width ratio of a flag is 2:3 (therefore, 2 inches high by 3 inches wide). If the flag is 10 inches high, how wide should the flag be?

2. Using the original pancakes recipe, change the ratio to make 20 servings.

6.3 DIRECT PROPORTION

Proportion is used to describe how amounts are related to each other. In direct proportion, as one amount increases the second amount increases, or as one decreases the other one also decreases at a set rate. Two things are considered in direct proportion if when plotting them on a graph you get a straight line through the origin (the corner of the graph).

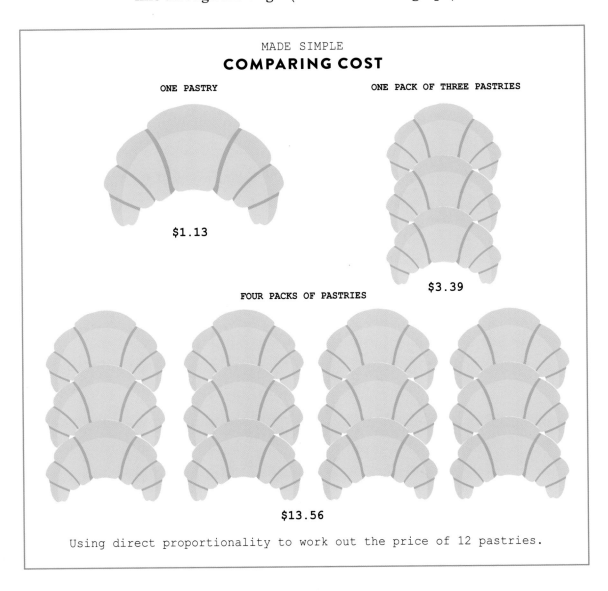

MADE SIMPLE
COMPARING COST

ONE PASTRY

ONE PACK OF THREE PASTRIES

$1.13

$3.39

FOUR PACKS OF PASTRIES

$13.56

Using direct proportionality to work out the price of 12 pastries.

Direct proportion can be used to solve problems if you remember the rule: "divide for one then multiply for all." For example: a car factory makes 93,800 cars each week, or every 7 days. How many cars are made in just 2 days? Start by dividing by 7 to find out how many cars are made per day: 93,800 ÷ 7 = 13,400. Then multiply that by 2 for how many cars are made in 2 days: 13,400 × 2 = 26,800. Therefore, 26,800 cars are made in 2 days.

Applying to cost

As food items are often sold in packs of more than one, direct proportion can be helpful in figuring out the price of one item and then scaling up. For example, three pastries cost $3.39, so how much will 12 pastries cost? Again, start by dividing to find the cost of one pastry: $3.39 ÷ 3 = $1.13. Now multiply this by the number of pastries we are interested in, 12: $1.13 × 12 = $13.56.

The symbol for direct proportion is ∝. If we say A is directly proportional to B, we can write it as A ∝ B. In the above examples we can state 3 pastries ∝ $3.39, once divided it becomes 1 pastry = $1.13, and we can use this equation to find the cost of any number of pastries.

ANSWER THIS

1. 6 bananas cost $1.80, so how much will 10 bananas cost?

2. Sally walks 49 miles a week, so how many miles does she walk in a year (non-leap year)?

3. John reads 8 books in 2 months, so how many does he read in 12 months?

COMPOUND GROWTH AND DECAY

You are likely to come across compound growth and decay in real life when looking at compound interest. Interest is an amount of money (a percentage) added to a bigger sum of money usually once a year or once a month. The amount added, or interest, is calculated as a percentage of the bigger amount. Compound interest is different to simple interest as the percentage increase is applied to the new total amount, or balance, each year, rather than just the same percentage of the starting balance.

It is important to understand compound growth when it comes to bank accounts and buying a house, so you can find the best deal. For example, Morgan has $100 in her bank account. Each year, the bank will add 5% interest to the total balance. 5% of $100 is $5, so in the first year, the bank

FACT

Most things purchased today will suffer from either compound or simple decay as they age, but there are a few things other than houses or apartments that increase in value. High-end art, Burgundy wine, Rolex watches, and diamonds are all known to increase in value with age.

MADE SIMPLE
GROWTH AND DECAY

Compound increase in house prices, and decay in how much a car is worth.

added $5, now she has $105. The next year, the bank adds 5% of the new total balance $105: 5% of $105 is $5.25. $5.25 is now added, and the new total at the end of the second year is $110.25. This carries on, with the bank adding 5% of the new balance each year.

Decreasing value

In compound decay, the numbers go down. Often when you buy a new car, it drops in worth. Cordelia just bought a new car for $21,000. The first year she has the car it decreases by 10%, then by 5% every year after. At the end of the first year, it will be $2,100 (10%) less; it is now worth $18,900. From now on, it goes down by 5% on the new price each year: at the end of the second year it has decreased by 5% of $18,900: $945, and becomes worth $17,995. At the end of the next year, it decreases at 5% of $17,995 (the new total): $899.75, and becomes worth $17,095.25, and so on.

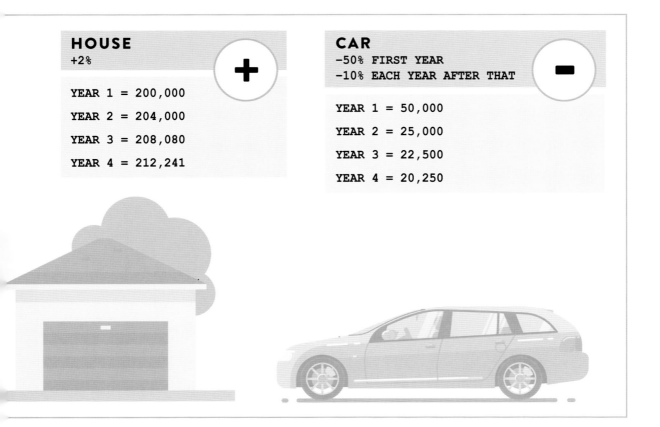

HOUSE
+2%

YEAR 1 = 200,000

YEAR 2 = 204,000

YEAR 3 = 208,080

YEAR 4 = 212,241

CAR
−50% FIRST YEAR
−10% EACH YEAR AFTER THAT

YEAR 1 = 50,000

YEAR 2 = 25,000

YEAR 3 = 22,500

YEAR 4 = 20,250

6.5 PRESSURE, FORCE, AREA

Pressure is a measure of how much force is applied over a given area: Pressure = ^{FORCE}/_{AREA}. More force leads to more pressure, but more area leads to less pressure. Pressure is directly proportional to force and inversely proportional to area (as one increases, the other decreases). Pressure is often measured in Pascals (Pa): the force of 1 Newton applied over 1 square meter produces a pressure of 1 Pa. Pressure is also measured in pounds per square inch (psi).

It's important to remember that force and pressure are not the same thing, and this is where some people get confused. **Force** is the interaction or impact of an object against another, such as the push or pull of a motion, and it is measured in Newtons. **Pressure** is how much that force will be "felt" due to the area it covers. For example, snow shoes have a larger surface area than normal shoes, which means the force is applied to a larger area and therefore less pressure is applied, meaning the wearer's feet do not sink into the snow as much.

FACT

Psi is the most common measure for car-tire pressure. Manufacturers will recommend the pressure of your tires on your car on a sticker (usually in a doorjamb), and it may differ depending on whether there's a couple of people in the car or if it's fully loaded. The recommended pressure is usually around 30 to 35 psi.

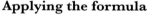

Applying the formula

The formula for pressure is: Pressure (P) = Force (F)/Area (A). If force is in Newtons (N) and area in m^2, the pressure is written in Pascals (Pa). For example, a force of 33 N is acting over an area of 11 m^2; to calculate pressure, divide force by area: $33 \div 11 = 3$ N/m^2, or 3 Pa. If the force is measured in pounds (i.e. weight) and the area is in^2, the unit for pressure in this case is pounds per square inch (psi). For example, a force of 20 pounds acts over an area of 5 square inches; divide the force by area: $20 \div 5 = 4$, therefore the pressure is 4 psi.

If you have pressure and area, you can calculate the force being applied by rearranging the equation or using the illustrated triangle. When finding out force, cover the F—you are left with pressure × area. When calculating area, cover the A and you are left with force ÷ pressure.

FORMULA TRIANGLE

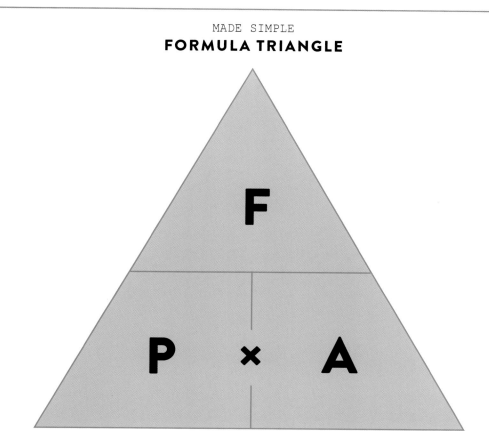

Triangle illustrating the relationship between force (F), pressure (P), and area (A). Cover up the measure you want to find and that will tell you what to do with the other two measures.

ANSWER THIS

1. A force of 30 N is applied to a surface of 4 m^2. What is the pressure applied to the surface?

2. If a force of 250 pounds is applied to an area of 5 square inches, what is the pressure?

3. If the force is 8 N and the pressure is 4 Pa, what is the area the force is being applied over?

4. If the area a force is being applied to is 10 square inches and the pressure is 3.5 psi, what is the force being applied?

6.6 PERCENTAGE CHANGE

When changing a number based on a percent or portion of the original total amount, it can be a gain or loss to the original amount. To calculate using percentages, convert the percentage to a multiplier and times the original amount by it. The earlier chapter on converting percentages to decimal numbers will come in handy here.

MADE SIMPLE
INCREASE IN VALUE

To find the 66% increase, multiply the original amount by 1.66 (as it's 166% of the original price).

Vintage coat
worth 66% more

ORIGINAL PRICE
= **$200**

NEW PRICE
= **$322**

The quickest way to calculate percentage change is to times it by a multiplier. In order to do that, you have to change the percent into a decimal number, which is the multiplier. If there is a percentage gain or increase, it is relatively easy, as you add 100% (as you want to keep the original amount). Then just turn it into a decimal number, which is the same as dividing by 100. (Remember: when you divide by 100, you move the decimal point two places to the left). If there is a 73% increase, add 100%: 173%, change the percentage into the multiplier: 1.73, and multiply this by the original amount.

Bob has a vintage coat that was $200 when he bought it. It has increased in price due to its age and style, and is now worth 66% more. To work out the multiplier, add 100%: 166%, and then divide by 100: 1.66. Now calculate $200 × 1.66 = $322. Bob's coat is now worth $322.

Working out loss

When we have a percentage loss or decrease, we aren't keeping the original amount, so we don't add the 100%. To convert it to a multiplier, minus the percent from 100%, then divide by 100 to get a decimal number. Then, as above, multiply by the multiplier. For example, Jaden had a bag of 180 smarties, he ate 20% yesterday, so how many does he have left? As it is a decrease, first take 20% away from 100%: 80%. Now turn 80% into a multiplier by dividing by 100: 0.80. Lastly, multiply the multiplier by the original amount: 180 × 0.8 = 144 smarties.

1. Convert a 50% gain into a multiplier:
   a. 0.05
   b. 0.50
   c. 0.15
   d. 1.50

2. What is a 39% loss as a multiplier?
   a. 0.39
   b. 3.90
   c. 0.61
   d. 1.61

3. A Eucalyptus tree had 10 flowers on it yesterday, but today the number has risen by 20%:
   a. What is the multiplier to calculate the new amount?
   b. How many flowers are on it today?

4. A household produced 40 pounds of trash last week, but decreased it by 15% this week:
   a. What is the multiplier to calculate the new amount?
   b. How much trash did it produce this week?

MAPS AND SCALE DRAWINGS

Maps are scaled down versions of the real world—a life-size map would not be practical! A map uses a scale most appropriate for its size; for example, a map of the whole USA might be 1 inch = 300 miles, where 1 inch represents 300 miles, but a map of central Pittsburgh may be 1 inch = 800 feet. Maps show scale either through words: e.g., 1 inch = 300 miles, or through a ruler line marked with distance, and you then have to measure the line.

CALCULATING DISTANCES

Maps are useful when charting routes on a smaller scale and being able to calculate distances.

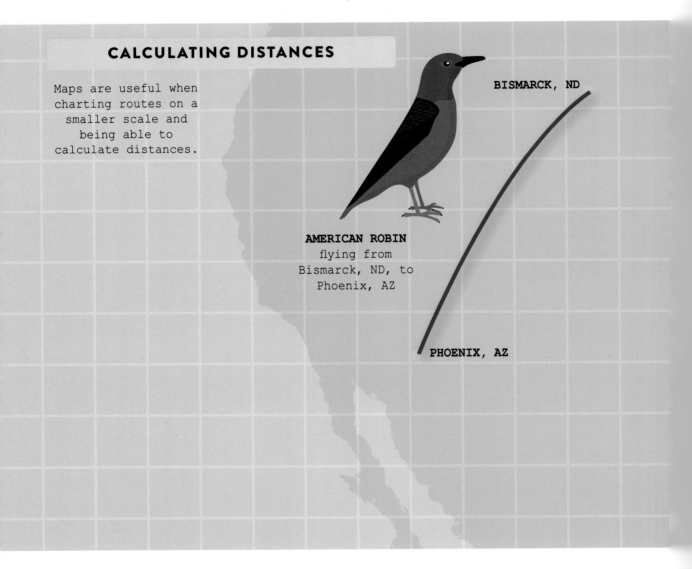

BISMARCK, ND

AMERICAN ROBIN
flying from
Bismarck, ND, to
Phoenix, AZ

PHOENIX, AZ

1. If a map is drawn to the scale 1 inch = 300 miles, what would be the length of a 1,200-mile road on the map?

2. On a map with a scale of 1 inch = 7 yards, how far (in inches) would two objects be if they were 49 yards away from each other?

3. On a map scaled at 1 cm = 2 km, in a car route shown as 5 cm long, how far did that car actually go?

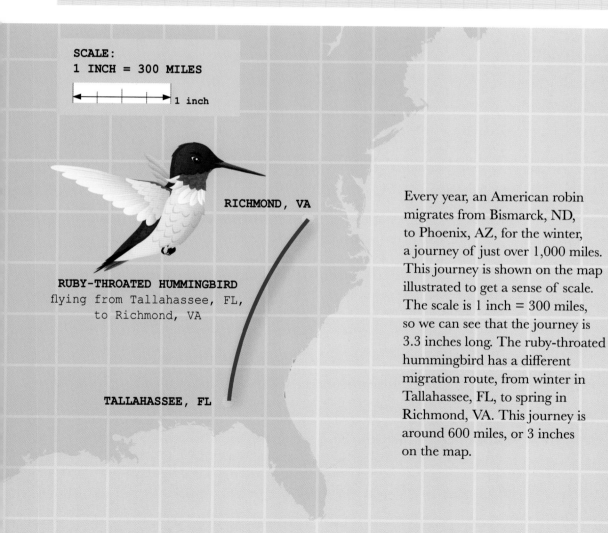

SCALE:
1 INCH = 300 MILES

1 inch

RICHMOND, VA

RUBY-THROATED HUMMINGBIRD
flying from Tallahassee, FL,
to Richmond, VA

TALLAHASSEE, FL

Every year, an American robin migrates from Bismarck, ND, to Phoenix, AZ, for the winter, a journey of just over 1,000 miles. This journey is shown on the map illustrated to get a sense of scale. The scale is 1 inch = 300 miles, so we can see that the journey is 3.3 inches long. The ruby-throated hummingbird has a different migration route, from winter in Tallahassee, FL, to spring in Richmond, VA. This journey is around 600 miles, or 3 inches on the map.

6.8 DENSITY AND SPEED

Density and speed are both proportional measures. Density is found by dividing mass by volume, and it is directly proportional to mass and indirectly proportional to volume. Speed is the distance traveled per unit of time, such as miles per hour or meters per second. Speed is directly proportional to distance and indirectly proportional to time.

FACT

On Earth, the densest-known material is osmium, a metallic element at 23 g/cm³. The least dense material is aerographite, which is 0.2 mg/cm³, or 0.0002 g/cm³, for comparison's sake.

Density = $^{\text{MASS}}/_{\text{VOLUME}}$

When using formula triangles, cover up the thing you want to find out and write down what's left, then put in the values. For example, to find volume, cover up the V and you are left with M over D, which is mass divided by density. The units for density depend on the units used for mass and volume; if pounds and cubic inches are used, then it is pound per cubic foot. If the mass is measured in grams and volume in cm³, then it is g/cm³. The denser an object, the heavier it feels for its size. If Ernest picks up a rock with a volume of 15 cubic inches, or in³, and a mass of 30 pounds, how dense is the rock? Remember: density = mass divided by volume, so the rock is 30/15 = 2 pounds/in³.

Speed = $^{\text{DISTANCE}}/_{\text{TIME}}$

We can create a formula triangle for this formula as well, as shown in the illustration. To find the distance, cover the D and see speed × time. Similarly, the units for speed depend on the units used for distance and time. If distance is measured in km and time in hours, then it is km/hr. If distance is measured in miles and time in hours, then it is miles/hr. Ethel-May takes 2 hours to drive to see her son in Kent, OH, which is 86 miles away. To calculate her average speed, divide the distance by the time: 86 ÷ 2 = 43. Her average speed is 43 m/hr.

MADE SIMPLE
FORMULA TRIANGLES

Formula triangles are the easiest ways to remember density and speed formulas.

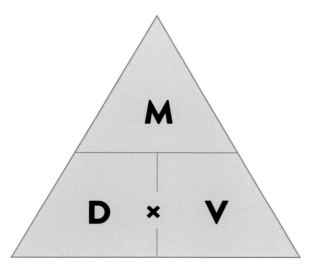

Triangle showing the relationship between density (D), mass (M), and volume (V)

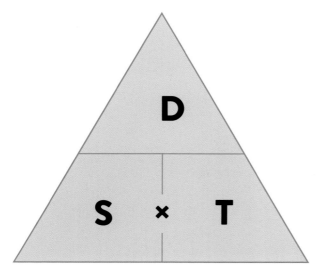

Triangle illustrating the relationship between speed (S), distance (D), and time (T)

1. If the mass of an object is 230 pounds and its volume is 20 cubic feet, what is its density?

2. Gold has a density of about 20 g/cm^3. If a gold bar has a volume of 20 cm^3, what is the mass of the ingot in grams?

3. If a bus traveled at 60 miles/hr for 3 hours, how far did it go?

4. A sphinx moth flies 7 miles in 14 minutes, so what is its speed (in miles/minute)?

RATE OF CHANGE, RATIO, AND PROPORTION

1. **What is the ratio of nonfiction to fiction books if there are 50 nonfiction books and 42 fiction books?**

   a. 25:21

   b. 100:50

   c. 92:51

   d. 92:42

2. **A dress has a ratio of white sequins to black sequins of 4:5. If there are 100 white sequins, how many black sequins are there on the dress?**

   a. 40

   b. 50

   c. 100

   d. 125

3. **The price of kiwi fruit is directly proportional to the number you purchase. Eight kiwi fruit cost $8.80, so how much will 20 kiwi fruit cost?**

   a. $16

   b. $20

   c. $22

   d. $30

4. **Lucy bought a house for $300,000. It increases by 5% each year. How much will it be worth after the second year?**

   a. 330,000

   b. 310,000

   c. 330,750

   d. 300,010

5. **George bought a new computer for $500 but it will lose 20% of its value each year. How much is it worth after three years?**

   a. $200

   b. $450

   c. $412

   d. $256

6. **A force of 72 N is applied to a surface of 6 m². Calculate the pressure being applied to the surface.**

   a. 12 Pa

   b. 72 Pa

   c. 10 Pa

   d. 6 Pa

7. **During winter a tree with 250 leaves loses 42% of its leaves:**

   a. What is the equivalent multiplier for 42% loss?

   b. How many leaves are left?

8. **A large ice cube weighs 9 pounds and has a volume of 3 in³. What is its density?**

   a. 9 pounds per in³

   b. 3 pounds per in³

   c. 3 pounds per ft³

   d. 3 pounds per in

9. **Fill in the speed, distance, time triangle below:**

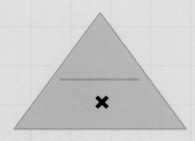

Answers on page 214

SIMPLE SUMMARY

Rate, ratio, and proportion are all ways to describe how one value relates to another value in some way. Rate of change is how values change over time (for example), ratio is how values relate to each other, and proportion is how values relate to the total.

- Ratios are a way of describing a relationship between two numbers; they are used to compare two or more things when items are shared unequally or there are an unequal number of objects in multiple groups.

- Ratios tell us the relative proportions of each ingredient, for example, and if we want to increase that ingredient, we need to also increase the other ingredients by the right amount.

- Direct proportion can be used to solve problems if you remember the rule: "divide for one then multiply for all."

- Compound interest is different to simple interest as the percentage increase is applied to the new total amount, or balance, each year, rather than just the same percentage of the starting balance.

- Pressure = $^{FORCE}/_{AREA}$ and is directly proportional to force and inversely proportional to area (as one increases, the other decreases).

- Percentage change is changing a number based on a percent or portion of the original total amount.

- Maps show scale either through words: e.g., 1 inch = 300 miles, or through a ruler line marked with distance, and you then have to measure the line.

- Density = $^{MASS}/_{VOLUME}$ and Speed = $^{DISTANCE}/_{TIME}$.

7

ALGEBRA: WHEN MATH IS MORE THAN NUMBERS

Algebra is the use of symbols and letters in place of numbers to create formulas, equations, and expressions. In this chapter you will learn how algebra can be used for problem solving, how to write formulas, the art of factorizing and multiplying out brackets, and how to describe patterns in number sequences.

WHAT YOU WILL LEARN

Using symbols

Using and writing formulas and expressions

Simplifying terms

Multiplying out brackets

Factorizing

Using formulas to solve problems

Patterns and sequences

7.1 USING SYMBOLS

Math isn't always just about numbers: letters and symbols have been part of math for as long as it's been around. This type of math is known as algebra, which uses symbols in place of values, and is most commonly applied in two ways: 1) to work out an unknown number; 2) in equations to describe relationships between different things.

Sometimes we don't know the value of something but are given information that may help. For example, if you add 10 to the number of eggs in the chicken coop, you get 25. To work out how many eggs there are, you would first assign the number of eggs a letter or symbol. We will use X for eggs, and then put it in an equation, X + 10 = 25:

$$X + \bullet\bullet\bullet\bullet\bullet\bullet\bullet\bullet\bullet\bullet = \begin{matrix}\bullet\bullet\bullet\bullet\bullet\bullet\bullet\bullet\bullet\bullet\bullet\bullet\bullet\\\bullet\bullet\bullet\bullet\bullet\bullet\bullet\bullet\bullet\bullet\bullet\bullet\end{matrix}$$

To work out *X*, we find out how much we would have to add to 10 to get 25:

$$X = 25 - 10$$

Total 25 eggs

minus 10 eggs

X equals 15, so there are 15 eggs.

ANSWER THIS

1. What is X in: X + 11 = 33?
   a. 33
   b. 11
   c. 20
   d. 22

2. Find the value of Y when 5Y = 60.
   a. 5
   b. 12
   c. 13
   d. 6

3. In the garden there are footballs and tennis balls, 11 in total. If F stands for footballs and T for tennis balls, which of the following equations is correct?
   a. F + T = 11
   b. F − T = 11
   c. FT = 11
   d. F + 11 = T

Let's try a more complicated example: You have picked 64 strawberries, which fills 8 boxes. Each box contains the same number of strawberries. You want to know how many strawberries fit in each box. Again, firstly assign a letter to the unknown value, in this example, the number of strawberries in the box, or Y. We know that 8 boxes of Y strawberries equals 64 strawberries. So our equation is $8 \times Y = 64$. When using algebra, we don't use the multiplication sign between numbers and letters, so it becomes $8Y = 64$. To find Y, find the number that 8 multiplies by to get 64:

WORKING WITH ALGEBRA

$$8 \times Y = 64 \text{ or } 8Y = 64$$
$$Y = 64 \div 8 \qquad Y = 8$$

There are 8 strawberries per box.

Describing relationships

Algebra is often used in equations where the relationship between subjects is fixed, i.e., it stays the same but the numbers may change. X and Y are the most commonly used letters but any can be used. For example, each year at Finley's party, he has 20 sandwiches; there are tuna sandwiches and cucumber sandwiches. There will always be 20 sandwiches in total, but the number of tuna or cucumber sandwiches varies each year. Similar to the earlier examples, we give letters or symbols to the unknown amounts, i.e., the number of each type of sandwich. Let's use T as the symbol for tuna sandwiches and C for cucumber sandwiches. If we add each type together, it totals 20, so this can be written as:

$$T + C = 20$$

If we know how many cucumber sandwiches there are, we can then use the equation to work out how many tuna sandwiches we need. If one year there are 13 tuna sandwiches, we put that in place of the T, so:

$$13 + C = 20$$

and work out what is left:

$$C = 20 - 13 = 7$$

7.2 USING AND WRITING FORMULAS

Formulas are created and used for calculations that are often carried out. They are used in finding areas and volumes or converting units. Knowing how to write and use formulas is an important skill. For example, an electrician will often apply a "callout" fee and an hourly rate; having a formula means he can calculate the cost of job more quickly.

Letters or symbols can be used to write general rules as equations. These general rules can then be applied in a multitude of circumstances. The first step when writing an algebraic or letter formula is to write out the calculation in words, then substitute the words for letters of your choosing. For example, to look at the total price of hotdogs with different prices and for different numbers of hotdogs: using letters, write a general rule of total price (T) = number of hotdogs (n) x price of hotdogs (H), or T = H × n, or T=Hn.

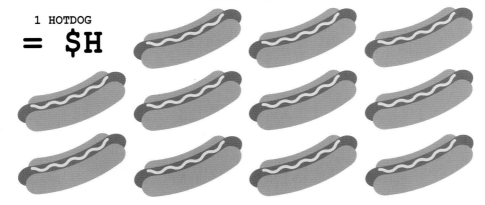

MADE SIMPLE
APPLYING FORMULA

To work out the total cost of these hotdogs, use the formula shown.

1 HOTDOG
= $H

Total price of hotdogs (T) = number of hotdogs (n) × price of hotdog (H)

Formulas or rules for calculations found earlier in the book, such as area or perimeter, can also be written. Like the example above, put the calculation into words: Perimeter of a square = length × 4; and then substitute in letters for the words: P = L × 4, or P = 4L. Area of a square = length × length, becomes A = L².

Complex formulas

Some formulas can be complicated, but writing out the calculation in words first will help to clarify them. Using the electrician example above: Total cost = call out fee + cost per hour × number of hours. Substitute letters in to become: $T = C + H \times n$, which becomes $T = C + Hn$. Depending on the electrician, these rates may vary—for example, Elsa's callout fee is \$50, and the cost per hour is \$20, so her formula becomes: $T = 50 + 20n$. Elsa calculates that the cost of a 5-hour job is $T = 50 + 20 \times 5 = \$150$.

FORMULAS IN PRACTICE

Tradespeople often use a simple formula to work out how much to charge their customers based on how long the job takes.

SPARKS ELECTRICIANS

BILL

Callout fee.................$50

Hourly rate.......$20 per hour

Time..................5 hours

TOTAL....................**$150**

Total cost (T) = call out fee (C) + cost per hour (H) × number of hours (n).

ANSWER THIS

1. A worker's pay (W) is dependent upon the number of hours worked (n), the rate per hour (R), and a one-off bonus (B). Try and write a formula to work out the worker's pay (W).

2. What is the formula for the area of a triangle where A = area, H = height, and B = base?

3. At lunch, Rick has one burger costing $4 and a few drinks, each costing $2. Write a formula for the total price (T) of his lunch.

In algebra, letters or symbols are used to stand for values that may change or are unknown. A term is a letter or number on its own within the formula or expression, such as 4x or 7. An expression is a set of terms linked using the operations +, −, ×, or ÷.

An expression is different from an equation as it doesn't contain an equal sign. An equation states that two expressions are the same, e.g., an algebraic formula might state that 5a + 3 = 6t, whereas an expression will just have one or more terms. Expressions can be written in the same way as formulas, by writing it out in words first. Your teacher buys p packs of pencils and e boxes of erasers. There are 7 pencils in each pack and 9 erasers in each box. The number of pencils is the number in each pack multiplied by the number of packs: 7 × p, which can be written as 7p. The number of erasers bought is the number of erasers in each box multiplied by the number of boxes: 9 × e, or 9e. The number of pencils and erasers purchased is 7p + 9e.

FACT

We may want, or find it useful, to write expressions to find the area of a square or the volume of a cube. The area of a square is length (x) times itself, the expression for area is just x^2. The volume of a cube is the length (x) times itself twice, so the expression for volume would be x^3.

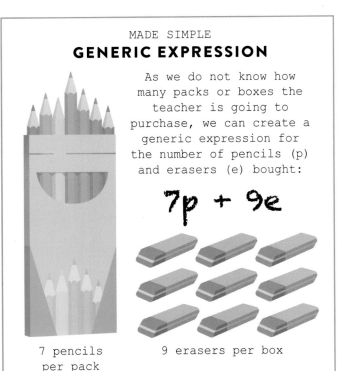

MADE SIMPLE
GENERIC EXPRESSION

As we do not know how many packs or boxes the teacher is going to purchase, we can create a generic expression for the number of pencils (p) and erasers (e) bought:

$$7p + 9e$$

7 pencils per pack

9 erasers per box

AGE-OLD EXPRESSION

A common expression question is regarding ages of three individuals. For example, we get told that Rene is n years old. Max is 3 years younger than Rene. Lastly, Amanda is half Max's age. Start by writing an expression for Rene's age in years: n. Then as Max is 3 years younger, the expression for his age is: n – 3. Lastly, Amanda's age is half of Max's, so take his expression and divide by 2: (n–3) ÷ 2.

RENE
n YEARS OLD

MAX
(n–3)

AMANDA
(n–3)/2

Knowing the relationship between the ages, we can write a set of expressions to work out the ages once we are told what n equals.

ANSWER THIS

Write your answers as an expression:

1. Bill won x number of dollars in a game, but he paid $50 to enter, so how much money did he make overall?

2. Michele made 10 chocolate cupcakes and b blueberry muffins; how many items did she make overall?

3. Zunaira was setting up 200 chairs and t tables, so how many chairs were at each table?

7.4 SIMPLIFYING TERMS

A term is a letter, symbol, or number (or combination thereof) on its own within the formula, such as 2n or 9. If the similar terms (such as lots of "x"s) are found in multiple places in the expression or equation, they may be grouped together to simplify the expression or equation. This is known as simplifying terms.

It is important for equations and expressions to be as simplified as possible, as this leaves less room for error: the more calculations made, the more likely an error. A simple example is finding the perimeter of a square with lengths (L). The perimeter is L + L + L + L, which can be simplified to 4L. To find the perimeter of a rectangle with length L and width D would be W + L + W + L. Now we can group the similar terms together, the Ws and the Ls, to become 2W + 2L.

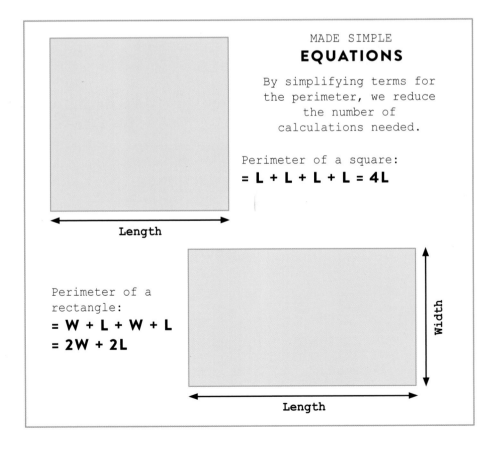

Length

MADE SIMPLE
EQUATIONS

By simplifying terms for the perimeter, we reduce the number of calculations needed.

Perimeter of a square:
= L + L + L + L = 4L

Perimeter of a
rectangle:
= W + L + W + L
= 2W + 2L

Width

Length

In the expression $10n + 7n - 2n$, the variable in each term is n, so we can group them all together and simplify the expression in order: $10n + 7n = 17n$, $17n - 2n = 15n$.

You can only simplify with like terms, such as all "n"s. However, if there are squared versions and non-squared versions of the same letter, these cannot be combined to be simplified in additions and calculations. For example, in $6x^2 + 2x + 5x$, the x^2 is considered a different term from the x, so the simplified expression is $6x^2 + 7x$.

With multiplications, multiply the numbers first and then the letter. In $6y \times 2y$, multiply the 6 by 2 to get 12, and the y by y to get y^2, then combine them so it becomes $12y^2$.

FACT

Remember to carry out the calculations according to BIDMAS or PEMDAS when simplifying, otherwise you may change the outcome of the equation or expression (see page 38).

MULTIPLYING SQUARED AND NONSQUARED

Calculating $6y \times 2y$

$6 \times 2 = 12$

$y \times y = y^2$

Now combine the two:

$12y^2$

ANSWER THIS

1. $x + y + x + y + x + y + y =$

2. $5x + 9x - 3x =$

3. $6c - 10b + a + 3c + 2b =$

4. $8e \times 3e + 7e =$

5. $3x \times 4x \times 5x =$

MULTIPLYING OUT BRACKETS

Some expressions or formulas have brackets, and as part of the calculation you will need to multiply the terms in the brackets by the term outside the brackets. You must multiply every term inside the brackets by the number or letter outside the brackets. If there are two terms inside, you must do two multiplications, so the number of terms tells you how many calculations you must do. This is a good way of checking you have done the right number.

When letters are multiplied together, they are just written next to each other, e.g., $y \times z = yz$. If a letter is multiplied by itself, it becomes that letter squared, e.g., $f \times f = f^2$. One mistake often made is thinking ab^2 is the same as $(ab)^2$—but they aren't! $ab^2 = a \times b \times b$, whereas $(ab)^2 = a \times a \times b \times b$. Lastly, if the number or letter outside the brackets is a minus, then you reverse all the signs inside the brackets (shown in the second example).

EXPANDING BRACKETS

When expanding or multiplying out brackets, multiply the term outside the bracket by everything inside the bracket. In this example, there are two terms inside the brackets, which means we must do two multiplications.

Expand:

$$9\,(2x + 4) = 9\,(2x + 4)$$

$$= 9 \times 2x + 9 \times 4$$

$$= 18x + 36$$

Expansion in action

Multiplying out brackets is also known as expanding brackets. If we have $4(2x + 3)$ and we want to expand, that means getting rid of the brackets. There are two terms inside the brackets, so we want to carry out two calculations: the outside terms multiplied by each of the inside terms.

1. $4 \times 2x = 8x$

2. $4 \times 3 = 12$

So, the expanded version is $8x + 12$.

Let's try and expand the next expression:
$-5(3x + 4y - 2)$. There are three terms, so do three multiplications, but note the number outside the brackets is a negative number, which has to be taken into account in our calculations:

1. $-5 \times 3x = -15x$

2. $-5 \times 4y = -20y$

3. $-5 \times -2 = 10$

Joined back up, it becomes $-15x - 20y + 10$.

FACTORIZING: INSERTING BRACKETS

Factorizing is the opposite of multiplying out brackets. With the latter, we are trying to get rid of the brackets, whereas with factorizing, we are putting brackets back in. Factorizing involves identifying common factors, so make sure you understand the factors section earlier (see page 24). Remember: A factor is a number that completely and exactly divides into a number.

When factorizing, first identify the biggest number that goes into all the terms (again, a term is just a number or letter in an expression). Place that number outside the brackets and open the brackets. Inside the brackets there will be new terms that you would use to multiply by the factor outside the brackets, to produce the original terms. For example, we want to factorize $8x - 6$. The largest factor common to both is 2, therefore this becomes the number outside the brackets: $2 (\ldots)$. Then look at how to get from the number outside the brackets to the first term— to get from 2 to $8x$, multiply by $4x$, so this is the new first term in the brackets: $2(4x\ldots)$. Lastly, to get from 2 to -6, multiply by -3: $2(4x - 3)$.

Letters as common factors
Sometimes the common factor is, in fact, a letter. For example, in $x^2 + 3x$, x is a common factor, as both terms divide by x. Similarly to numbers, if we remove the common factor, x, and place it outside the brackets, then identify the new terms: $x(\ldots)$. For the first term, to get from x to x^2, multiply by x, so this is the new first term inside the brackets: $x(x\ldots)$. For the second term, $+ 3x$, multiply x by 3, so 3 is the new second term: $x(x + 3)$.

ANSWER THIS

Factorize the following:
1. $2y - 14$

2. $12x + 8$

3. $x^2 + 8x$

4. $y^2 - 12y$

Factorize 5e + 15

$$5e + 15$$

Identify the number that is a common factor of both terms and/or the common letter.
In this case, 5 is a common factor to both, so place that outside a set of brackets with the original operation (+):

$$5 (+)$$

Fill in the brackets.
To get from the 5 outside the brackets to the original first term of 5e, multiply by e, so write that inside the brackets for the first term:

$$5 (e +)$$

Fill in the rest of the brackets
To get from the 5 outside the brackets to the original second term of 15, multiply by 3. Therefore, place 3 inside the brackets for the second term:

$$5 (e + 3)$$

NOTE: As there are two terms in the original expression, there must be two terms inside the brackets.

USING FORMULAS TO SOLVE PROBLEMS

Often, problems have many possible answers, or the one answer might not be that clear—formulas can help with these problems. Using a formula to solve problems is a strategy used in many areas in math, such as geometry, measurement, or algebra. Identifying and writing the most appropriate formulas are key.

Katie takes a trip to the craft store to buy coloring pencils (a pack costs $10), bottles of red paint ($5 per bottle), and paintbrushes ($2 each). She spends $50 and gets one pack of coloring pencils—the bottles of paint and paintbrushes add up to the rest. There are multiple options. The first thing to do is write a formula for total money spent.

BUILDING A FORMULA

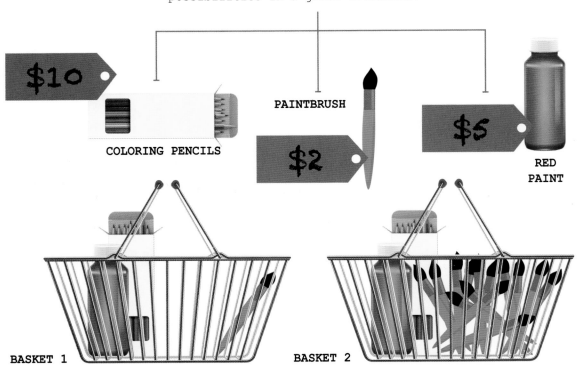

Using formulas, we can calculate all the possibilities in a given situation.

$10

COLORING PENCILS

PAINTBRUSH

$2

$5

RED PAINT

BASKET 1

BASKET 2

Remember, with formula building, write it out in words: Total cost = cost of coloring pencil packs × number of packs + cost of bottles of paint × number of bottles of paint + cost of paintbrushes × number of paintbrushes. If C = coloring pencils, P = number of bottles of paint, and B = number of brushes, the equation becomes:

$$\$50 = 10C + 5P + 2B$$

We know the cost of the coloring pencils as she only bought one, so it is $10. Minus that from both sides:

$$50 - 10 = 10 + 5P + 2B - 10$$
$$40 = 5P + 2B$$

Now, try out numbers to see which pairs of bottles and paints add up to $40. The best place to start is to make one of the P or B equal 1 and then go from there. Let's say only one bottle of paint was purchased, so it becomes:

$$40 = 5 + 2B$$

So, we minus 5 from both sides:

$$40 - 5 = 5 + 2B - 5$$

35 = 2B. P = 1 doesn't work, as 35 is not a multiple of 2, so we wouldn't get a whole number of paintbrushes. Next we try two bottles of paint, P = 2:

$$40 = (5 \times 2) + 2B$$
$$40 - 10 = 10 + 2B - 10$$
$$30 = 2B \qquad 15 = 2B$$

P = 2 does work, as that would leave enough money for 15 paintbrushes. Therefore, one possible option is that Katie bought 2 bottles of paint and 15 paintbrushes.

ANSWER THIS

There are two further possible combinations for the art supply example above. Figure them out.

PATTERNS AND SEQUENCES

Number sequences are lists of numbers that follow a particular pattern. Some patterns are quite simple, as long as you identify what's happening in each gap. There are a few different types of number sequences you should be able to identify: 1) a sequence where you add the same number each time; 2) a sequence where the same number is taken away each time; 3) add by a changing number; 4) multiply or divide by the same number each time.

A sequence of numbers is different to a random list of numbers. Some number sequences are clear, such as odd numbers (1, 3, 5, 7, etc.) or even numbers (2, 4, 6, 8, etc). Additionally, it is useful to know the sequence of square numbers: 1, 4, 9, 16, 25, 26, 49, 64, 81, 100 (that's 1–10 squared).

Investigating sequences

In sequences where it's not immediately obvious, the first thing to do is look at the difference between the numbers. For example, we are given the first five terms in a sequence, 2, 8, 14, 20, 26. The difference between each number is adding 6, so the rule for this particular sequence is: add 6 to the previous number. This helps us find the next terms in the sequence. If we want to find the twentieth term in this sequence, we would have added 6 twenty times from the first term (2), $20 \times 6 = 120 + 2 = 122$, therefore the twentieth term in the sequence is 122.

FINDING THE RULE

To find the rule for the sequence, look at the difference between each number. In this case it goes up by 6 from the previous number.

These are all the same

Rule: Add 6 to the previous term

If the rule for a sequence is minus 2 from the term before, and the first term is 200, we can easily find out the twelfth term by multiplying the difference each time by the number of terms: 12×2, and then minus this from the first term: $200 - 24 = 176$. Let's have a look at the following sequences and their rules:

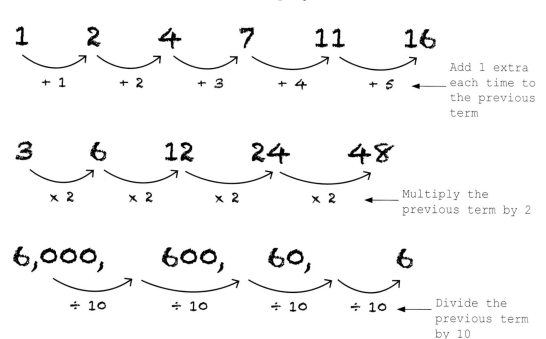

1   2   4   7   11   16

+ 1   + 2   + 3   + 4   + 5   ←—— Add 1 extra each time to the previous term

3   6   12   24   48

× 2   × 2   × 2   × 2   ←—— Multiply the previous term by 2

6,000,   600,   60,   6

÷ 10   ÷ 10   ÷ 10   ÷ 10   ←—— Divide the previous term by 10

ANSWER THIS

Find the rules in the following sequences:

1. 3, 7, 11, 15, 19, 23

2. 80, 71, 62, 53, 44, 35

3. 40, 20, 10, 5

4. 66, 65, 63, 60, 56

5. What is the 25th term in a sequence that starts at 6 and the rule is add 3 to the previous number?

ALGEBRA

1. Using the equation
   $98 - x = 54$, find x.

   a. 54

   b. 98

   c. 152

   d. 44

2. There are eight
   chocolate bars,
   each bar containing
   the same number of
   squares. If there are
   96 squares in total,
   what is the equation
   to find how many
   squares (S) on each
   chocolate bar?

   a. $8S = 96$

   b. $8 + S = 96$

   c. $8 \div S = 96$

   d. $96 + S = 8$

3. At brunch, Morty
   orders one bowl of
   cereal at $2.50 and a
   number (n) of coffees
   each costing around
   $4. Write a formula
   for the total price
   (T) of his breakfast.

   a. $T = 2.40 + 4$

   b. $T - 4 = 2.5$

   c. $Tn = 2.5$

   d. $T = 2.5 + 4n$

4. Amara was paid $200
   but had to pay t in
   taxes. How much did
   she have overall?

   a. $200 - t$

   b. $200 + t$

   c. $200t$

   d. $200 \div t$

5. Simplify
   $17x + 2x - 7y - 5x$

   a. $17x - 7y$

   b. $24x + 7y$

   c. $14x - 7y$

   d. $14x - 15y$

6. Simplify $2x \times 4x \times 3x$

   a. $24x^2$

   b. $24x$

   c. $24x^3$

   d. $9x^3$

7. Multiply out the
   brackets:
   $-3(10y + 2x)$

   a. $-30y - 2x$

   b. $-30y - 6x$

   c. $-30y + 6x$

   d. $-3y + 6x$

8. Factorize $3y + 27$

   a. $3(y + 27)$

   b. $3y + 9$

   c. $3(3y + 27)$

   d. $3(y + 9)$

9. Harriette buys a table
   (t) worth $100, chairs
   (c) at $25 each and
   seat cushions (s) at
   $10 each. She pays
   $400 in total and she
   buys a similar number
   of chairs and seat
   cushions.

   a. Write out a formula
   in words for the
   total cost of her
   shopping trip.

   b. Compose the formula
   using just letters
   and symbols this
   time.

   c. If Harriet bought 10
   seat cushions, how
   many chairs did she
   purchase?

10. Find the rule for
    the following
    sequence: 100, 92,
    84, 76, 68, 60.

11. What is the name of
    this sequence: 1, 4,
    9, 16, 25, 26, 49,
    64, 81, 100?

Answers on page 215

SIMPLE SUMMARY

Algebra is the use of symbols and letters in place of numbers to create formulas, equations, and expressions.

- Symbols in equations can be used to help find values for unknown amounts.

- Algebra is often used in equations where the relationship between subjects is fixed, i.e., it stays the same but the numbers may change.

- To write an algebraic or letter formula, write out the calculation in words, then substitute the words for letters of your choosing.

- A term is a letter or number on its own within the formula or expression, such as 4x or 7. An expression is a set of terms linked using the operations $+$, $-$, $\times$, or $\div$.

- If similar terms are found in multiple places in an expression or equation, they may be grouped together to simplify the expression or equation. This is known as simplifying terms.

- Some expressions or formulas will have brackets, and as part of the calculation you will need to multiply the terms in the brackets by the term outside the brackets.

- Factorizing involves putting brackets back in to an equation by identifying common factors.

- Formulas can help to identify all the possible answers to a problem.

- Number sequences are lists of numbers that follow a particular pattern.

8
STATISTICS AND PROBABILITY

Statistics and probability are used to calculate the chance of something happening. In this chapter, you will learn the basics about calculating the probability something will or won't happen, how to test this experimentally, and more complex probability rules.

WHAT YOU WILL LEARN

Probability

Counting outcomes

Probability that an outcome will not happen

Probability experiments

The And/Or rules

Tree diagrams

Conditional probability

Sets and Venn diagrams

LESSON 8.1

PROBABILITY: CALCULATING LIKELIHOODS

The chance, or probability, of an event happening can range from impossible to certainly occurring. You can describe probability as a fraction, a decimal, a percentage, or in words. All probabilities lie between 0 and 1 for fractions and decimals, and 0 and 100%. Probabilities are often shown on the scale illustrated here. The closer to 0 the probability is, the less likely it is; the closer to 1, the more likely it is to happen.

IMPOSSIBLE	UNLIKELY	EVEN	LIKELY	CERTAIN
0	0.25	0.5	0.75	1.0
0	¼	½	¾	1.0
0	25%	50%	75%	100%

The following formula can be used to calculate the likelihood or chance an outcome or event is to happen:

$$\text{Probability} = \frac{\text{outcome we are interested in}}{\text{total number of outcomes}}$$

For example, Jasper is an entomologist who collected 15 insects: 3 ladybugs, 7 bees, and 5 ants. Jasper is going to study them one at a time. What is the likelihood he is going to study an ant? To work that out, take the number of ants (5) over the number of total outcomes (15). So the probability that Jasper looks at an ant first is 5/15. Remember, we must simplify down fractions: 5/15 can be simplified to 1/3.

When writing probabilities, use a capital P followed by a word describing the outcome wanted in brackets. For example, the probability of getting an ant becomes P(ant). So we can write this as P(ant) = 1/3. If we want to see if he will pick an ant or a bee, we can add those probabilities together, so it becomes: P(ant or bee) = P(ant) + P(bee) = 5/15 + 7/15 = 12/15 = 4/5.

MADE SIMPLE
SAMPLE SPACE DIAGRAM

A diagram showing the possible outcomes when flipping two coins. We can see that there are four possible outcomes, and only one outcome where we get tails on both coins, so it is 1/4 chance of getting both tails.

COIN 1

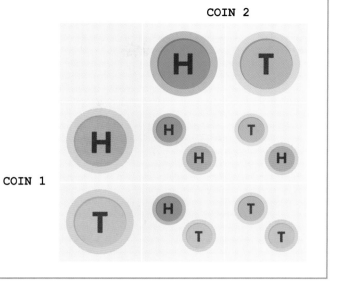

COIN 2

Probability of multiple outcomes at once

Sometimes two things are happening at once and we may have two outcomes occurring at the same time. For example, we flip two coins. Individually, each coin has a 1/2 chance of landing on tails, but the chance of both of them landing on tails is actually 1/4. We work this out by using sample space diagrams. Down the left hand-side we list all the possible outcomes for one part of the activity, i.e., coin 1, and across the top we list the possible outcomes for the second part. Now we can see there are 4 possible outcomes and only 1 where we get tails on both coins, so it is 1 out of 4—a 0.25 or 25% chance of getting tails on both coins.

ANSWER THIS

1. In her purse, Sarah has four different types of coins. She has 3 penny coins, 8 nickels, 10 dimes, and 9 dollar coins. What is the probability she picks a $1 coin?
   a. P($1) = 10/30
   b. P($1) = 1/30
   c. P($1) = 3/10
   d. P($1) = 1/

2. There are two coins, flipped at the same time. What is the likelihood one lands on heads and the other on tails?
   a. P(heads & tails) = 3/4
   b. P(heads & tails) = 2/2
   c. P(heads & tails) = 1/4
   d. P(heads & tails) = 1/2

8.2 COUNTING OUTCOMES

In probability questions or problems, the possible outcomes have to be identified first. Once the list of possible outcomes exists, it can be used to calculate probabilities of the particular outcomes we are interested in. If there is just one activity going on, such as rolling one die, it is relatively easy to list all the outcomes; however, it becomes more difficult when there are two or more activities occurring at the same time.

If there are two activities occurring at the same time, such as someone flipping a coin and rolling a die, a sample space diagram (see page 153) can be used to help us identify all the possible outcomes. For example, if two dice are rolled and the scores added up, what are all the possible outcomes (see illustration below)? There are 36 outcomes, although some of the totals are repeated.

MADE SIMPLE

OUTCOMES FOR SUM OF TWO DICE

The sample space diagram shows all the possible values from the sum of dice 1 (on the top) and dice 2 (along the side). We can see that there are 36 possible outcomes.

		DICE 1				
		1	2	3	4	5	6
DICE 2	1	2	3	4	5	6	7
	2	3	4	5	6	7	8
	3	4	5	6	7	8	9
	4	5	6	7	8	9	10
	5	6	7	8	9	10	11
	6	7	8	9	10	11	12

If there are more than two activities occurring, however, we may be able to use the "product rule" to count outcomes. If the number of outcomes is large, this is also a helpful way of calculating all possible outcomes accurately. The product rules state: the number of outcomes from a combination of activities is the same as the number of outcomes from each individual activity multiplied by each other.

	DICE 1	DICE 2	DICE 3	DICE 4	DICE 5
OUTCOME 1	1	1	1	1	1
OUTCOME 2	1	1	1	1	2
OUTCOME 3	1	1	1	1	3
OUTCOME 4	1	1	1	1	4
OUTCOME 5	1	1	1	1	5

When more than two activities are occurring, we can use the product rule to calculate the total number of possible outcomes—listing them would take too long!

For example, Andrew rolls five 6-sided dice and wants to calculate the total possible outcomes combinations. With the product rule, we would multiply by the possible outcomes for dice 1 by outcomes for dice 2 by outcomes for dice 3, and so on. There are six possible outcomes for each dice (as there are six sides), so this becomes: $6 \times 6 \times 6 \times 6 \times 6 = 7776$ possible outcomes.

Andrew is then asked to find the number of ways to get just odd numbers on the dice. This time there are only three outcomes per dice: 1, 3, or 5. As there are five dice, the possible outcomes where just odd numbers are rolled is: $3 \times 3 \times 3 \times 3 \times 3 = 243$. Now we know the number of outcomes with just odd numbers and the total possible outcomes, we can work out the probability that all the dice were odd when five 6-sided dice were rolled: $P(odd) = 243 \div 776 = 0.03$.

ANSWER THIS

1. Six fair coins are tossed:
a. Calculate the total number of possible outcomes.
b. Calculate the probability of always getting tails.

2. Four 6-sided dice are rolled:
a. Calculate the total number of possible outcomes.
b. What is the probability of only getting even numbers on each dice?

PROBABILITY THAT AN OUTCOME WILL NOT HAPPEN

Sometimes we are interested in the probability an outcome will *not* occur, and this involves an extra calculation or looking at the problem from a different angle. The probability that *any* outcome will occur is always 1; therefore, to find the probability that an event doesn't occur will be 1 minus the probability it does occur.

When we are talking about the probability of X *not* occurring, it is written with an apostrophe next to the event name: P(X'). The way to calculate the probability of something not occurring is to subtract it from the probability of anything occurring: P(X') = 1 − P(X).

For example, Abigail's school sold 2,000 tickets for the raffle. Abigail's family bought 30 tickets, so we know the probability she wins the raffle is 30/2000, so P(winning) = 0.015. To find the probability Abigail does not win (which, let's face it, is much more likely) is P(winning') = 1 − P(winning), which is P(winning') = 1 − 0.015 = 0.985. We can see Abigail is far more likely not to win the raffle than she is to win.

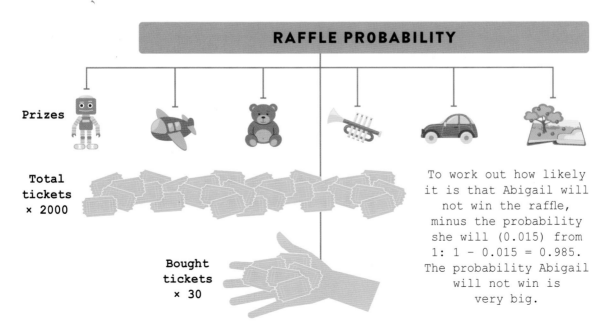

RAFFLE PROBABILITY

Prizes

Total tickets × 2000

Bought tickets × 30

To work out how likely it is that Abigail will not win the raffle, minus the probability she will (0.015) from 1: 1 − 0.015 = 0.985. The probability Abigail will not win is very big.

Multiple outcomes

Calculating the probability an event will not occur can appear confusing when there are multiple possible events or outcomes rather than just two (e.g., winning or not winning), but the principle is the same.

For example, Robert has a bag of 40 marbles: 12 red, 15 blue, 8 yellow, and 5 green. If Robert pulls a marble out of the bag, what is the probability it is not yellow? There are two ways of solving this: 1) Calculate the probability of getting a yellow marble and subtract that from one; or 2) Calculate the probability of getting all the other outcomes (add them up). Robert uses method 2): so, the probability of getting the other colors is $(12 + 15 + 5) \div 40 = 0.8$, P(yellow') = 0.8.

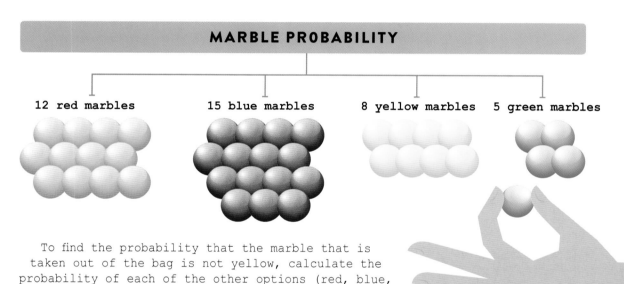

MARBLE PROBABILITY

12 red marbles 15 blue marbles 8 yellow marbles 5 green marbles

To find the probability that the marble that is taken out of the bag is not yellow, calculate the probability of each of the other options (red, blue, or green) and add them up. P(yellow') = 0.8.

ANSWER THIS

1. If the numbers 1 to 10 are placed in a hat, what is the probability that a 2 is not drawn?
   a. 0.10
   b. 0.20
   c. 1.00
   d. 0.90

2. A die is rolled: calculate the probability it does not land on 5.

3. Which is the correct notation for the probability the outcome Y will not happen?
   a. P(Y)
   b. P(Y!)
   c. P(Y')
   d. P(Yx)

PROBABILITY EXPERIMENTS

Sometimes outcomes are biased in one or many directions and, therefore, we may not get the expected outcome the number of times expected. Probability experiments are used to work out relative frequencies and the experimental probability of an outcome occurring. This allows us to take all biases into consideration and, if need be, account for them.

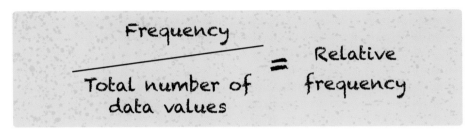

$$\frac{Frequency}{Total\ number\ of\ data\ values} = Relative\ frequency$$

Relative frequency, or experimental probability, of an event is the number of times the event occurs divided by the total number of trials (a trial is each time you try an activity, such as each time you flip a coin). By carrying out experiments, we can test if there are any biases and improve on the predicated probability of an outcome occurring.

FACT

Biased means some outcomes or events are more likely than others, if everything else is equal. A biased dice would roll some numbers more than others, despite the expected probability of each number being the same.

For example, Ernesto flips a coin. If there is no bias, then there is an equal chance, or probability, of him getting heads or tails: P(heads) = 0.5 and P(tails) = 0.5. However, if you have ever flipped a coin, you may know they can be biased, and repeatedly carrying out the trial (flipping a coin) will allow Ernesto to see the true frequency of getting tails (for example). Ernesto flips it 200 times and he gets heads 125 times and tails 75 times. The relative frequency of getting heads = 125 ÷ 200 = 0.625. The relative frequency of getting tails = 75 ÷ 200 = 0.375. Ernesto can see it is a biased coin, as if it was fair, he could expect to get heads 100 times and tails 100 times.

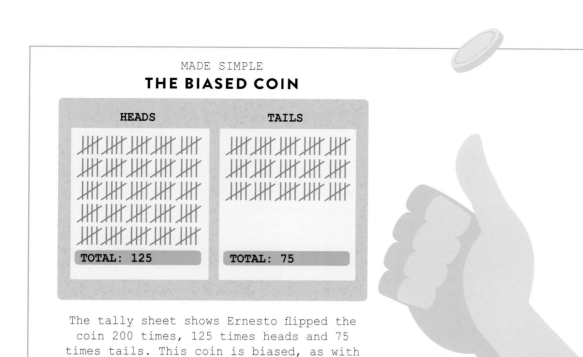

MADE SIMPLE
THE BIASED COIN

HEADS

TAILS

TOTAL: 125

TOTAL: 75

The tally sheet shows Ernesto flipped the coin 200 times, 125 times heads and 75 times tails. This coin is biased, as with a fair coin you would expect to get the same number of heads as tails.

Improving accuracy

Experimental probability grows more accurate the more trials or number of times the experiment is repeated. So, flipping a coin 200 times will give you a more accurate probability than just flipping it 10 times. In Ernesto's trials, he flips the coin a further 800 times (1,000 times in total). This time the coin lands on heads 546 times and tails 454 times. The relative frequency for heads now is 546 ÷ 1000 = 0.546 and for tails is 454 ÷ 1000 = 0.454. These relative frequencies are much closer to the expected probabilities and therefore the coin is not as biased as Ernesto previously thought.

ANSWER THIS

1. If a die is rolled 20 times and lands on 2 seven times, what is the relative frequency of rolling a 2?
   a. 0.35
   b. 0.65
   c. 0.7
   d. 0.20

2. If a coin is flipped 100 times and lands on tails 80 times, what is the relative frequency of getting tails?
   a. 0.60
   b. 0.20
   c. 0.80
   d. 1.00

8.5

THE AND/OR RULES

You may be asked to calculate the probability of two outcomes either occurring together or just one of them occurring. There are two easy-to-remember rules: the And rule for calculating when two outcomes *both* occur; and the Or rule for calculating the probability that *either* of the two outcomes occur.

An easy way to remember the And rule is that we see option 1 AND option 2 occurring. The probability of two events both happening at the same time is equal to the two individual probabilities multiplied by each other. (Note: this only works for independent outcomes, where one does not affect the other.) For example, Tanya has a bag which contains lots of marbles of different colors. She says the probability of getting a red marble is 0.3 (P(red) = 0.3) and the probability of getting a green marble is 0.1 (P(green) = 0.1). If one marble is taken out and then replaced, and another marble is taken out, what is the probability one will be green and the other is red? Using the above equation: P(green and red) = P(green) x P(red) = 0.1 × 0.3 = 0.03.

P(X <u>and</u> Y) = P(X) × P(Y)

AND RULE: Probability of events X and Y both occurring is equal to the probability of X multiplied by the probability of Y occurring.

 FACT　Two events are independent if the probability of one event happening doesn't affect the probability of the other happening. Events are dependent if one event happening affects the probability of another one occurring, such as removing a ball from a bag and not replacing it.

P(X or Y) = P(X) + P(B) – P(X and Y)

OR RULE: Probability of events X or Y occurring is equal to the probability of X added to the probability of Y minus the probability they both occur.

To calculate the probability that either one of two outcomes occurs, we use the Or rule. To remember this, just think we are saying either option 1 OR option 2 occurs. The probability of either events occurring is equal to the two separate probabilities added together minus the probability they both occur. If the events are mutually exclusive (i.e., they cannot occur at the same time), it is just the probability of each outcome added together. Using the same example as above, what is the probability that when a marble is removed from the bag it is either red or green? P(green or red) = P(green) + P(red) = 0.1 + 0.3 = 0.4.

ANSWER THIS

1. If two (fair) coins are tossed, what is the probability both show heads?
   a. 0.5
   b. 1.0
   c. 0.55
   d. 0.25

2. A bag contains 4 red balls, 3 yellow balls, and 5 orange balls. One ball is picked at random. Calculate the probability it's a red ball.

3. If a die is rolled and a coin is tossed, what is the probability of rolling a 4 and getting tails?
   a. 0.083
   b. 0.667
   c. 0.333
   d. 0.166

8.6 TREE DIAGRAMS

When you have a combination of events happening one after the other, tree diagrams can be very helpful for working out the probabilities of all the outcomes. In a tree diagram there is a set of branches for each activity, and branches at each stage for each outcome. Every branch is labeled with the probability on the branch line. Tree diagrams can be used for both independent and dependent events; they are particularly helpful at keeping track of probabilities in dependent outcomes.

Tree diagrams are named as they have a series of branches, like trees. On any set of branches that meet at a point (representing one trial or activity) the probabilities must add up to 1. To get the end probability, multiply all the probabilities along the branches to get there.

Using the tree diagram illustrated on the opposite page, it is possible to calculate a number of different combinations for the first and second marbles. To find the probability that both marbles are green: P(green and green) = $^3/_7 \times {}^3/_7 = {}^9/_{49}$. To find the probability that the first marble is red and the second one is green, follow the first branch for red and then the second green branch: P(red then green) = $^4/_7 \times {}^3/_7 = {}^{12}/_{49}$.

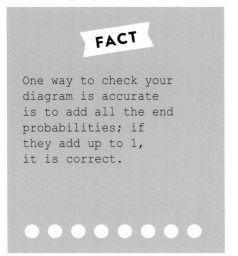

FACT

One way to check your diagram is accurate is to add all the end probabilities; if they add up to 1, it is correct.

Sometimes there are multiple possible routes, such as the probability of getting different colors each time, so outcome 1 could be green, then red, and outcome 2 could be red, then green. If this is the case, then calculate each route's probability and add them together. So P(green then red or red then green) = $^3/_7 \times {}^4/_7 + {}^4/_7 \times {}^3/_7 = {}^{24}/_{49}$.

MADE SIMPLE
THE TREE DIAGRAM

This tree diagram shows the possible combinations and the individual probabilities for a bag of marbles. This bag contains 3 green marbles and 4 red marbles.

One marble is removed at random and its color is identified before it is put back in the bag. This occurs twice. Note that the probabilities in the first marble add to 1 (a quick check to see if it is accurate).

1st marble

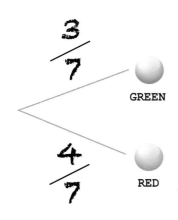

2nd marble

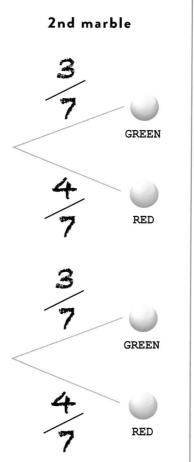

ANSWER THIS

Using the tree diagram above, calculate the following:

1. P(red and red) =
2. P(green then red) =
3. P(same colors both times*) =

*[Hint: P(red and red or green and green)]

8.7 CONDITIONAL PROBABILITY

Conditional probabilities are used for dependent events, which are when one outcome affects the probability of the second outcome occurring. This will usually be seen in questions or problems where items are not replaced, such as a bag of balls where one ball is removed but not replaced.

To calculate conditional probabilities, an adapted version of the And rule is used. The probability of events E and F both happening is equal to the probability of E occurring multiplied by the probability of F occurring, given that outcome E has already happened. The way to write this is:

$$P(E \underline{and} F) = P(E) \times P(F \underline{given} E)$$

Formula to calculate conditional probability
if event E occurs first and then event F.

ANSWER THIS

There are nine red cards and three yellow in a bag. One card is taken out at random and is not replaced (therefore, there is one fewer in the bag). Remember to write your answers in their simplest form (cancel down!).

1. What is the probability that the first card is red and the second card is yellow?
   a. 9/44
   b. 1/4
   c. 3/132
   d. 40/100

2. Calculate the probability that both cards are the same color.
   a. 1/11
   b. 7/12
   c. 13/22
   d. 9/11

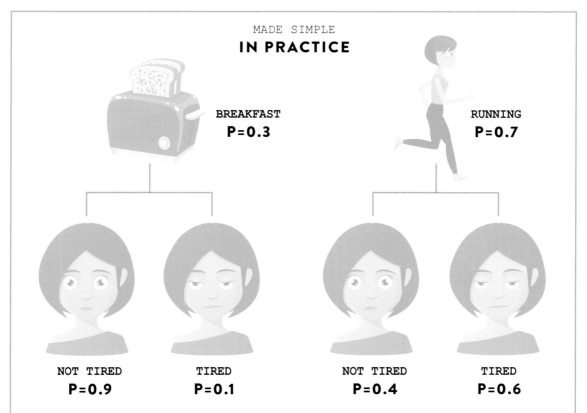

IN PRACTICE

BREAKFAST
P=0.3

RUNNING
P=0.7

NOT TIRED
P=0.9

TIRED
P=0.1

NOT TIRED
P=0.4

TIRED
P=0.6

The first thing Haleema does in the morning is either go for a run or have breakfast. The probability she goes for a run is 0.7. If she has breakfast, the probability she is not tired in the afternoon is 0.9. What is the probability that Haleema has breakfast and isn't tired in the afternoon? We want to find P(breakfast and isn't tired). The first thing to do is label the events: call "eating breakfast" outcome A, and "isn't tired" outcome B. To work out P(eating breakfast) = P(A) = 1 – 0.7 = 0.3. P(isn't tired, given she eats breakfast) = P(B given A) = 0.9. So the probability of Haleema eating breakfast and not being tired in the afternoon: P(A and B) = P(A) × P(B given A) = 0.3 × 0.9 = 0.27.

Changing probabilities

In the examples on page 163, if marbles are replaced each time, the events are independent and the probabilities do not change. If they are not replaced each time, the probabilities change each time and the events are dependent. For example, if there are 10 marbles to start with, the probabilities are out of 10; if one marble is removed and not replaced, the new probabilities are now out of 9.

8.8 SETS AND VENN DIAGRAMS

A set is a group of numbers, letters, or words. Venn diagrams are a way of showing sets in circles and squares. These diagrams are an interesting way of displaying data but can also be useful when calculating probabilities. This is probably the most common diagram you may see on social media, often used in a humorous way.

MADE SIMPLE
UNIVERSAL SET

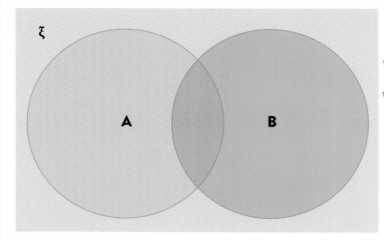

The Venn diagram represents the universal set (ξ—all the elements within the rectangle): the circle with A contains all the elements of set A; the circle with B contains all the elements of set B. If any elements are found in both sets, they are listed in the intersection.

FACT

The universal set is the group of things that all the elements of sets are selected from. It includes everything in the rectangle and is written as ξ.

A set is a collection of items, in this case numbers. Each of these items or numbers are known as elements. Sets are usually written as a list or description within curly brackets {}, for example {even numbers up to 20}, or {2, 3, 5, 7, 11, 13, 17, 19}. A Venn diagram illustrates whether elements from two or more sets overlap or are mutually exclusive. n(A) means the number of elements in set A, for example if A = {1, 7, 9, 13, 17, 21} then n(A) = 6. On a Venn diagram, sets are represented by their own circle containing their elements of the set.

Venn diagrams can be used to find probabilities. For example, students in school were asked if they liked math, music, both, or none. The findings are shown on the Venn diagram below. We can see how many students liked each subject, or none if the number is outside the circles. To find out the probability that a student picked at random liked math, add up all the numbers in the circle labeled "math" and divide by the total number of students. The total number of students is found by adding all the numbers on the Venn diagram, e.g., 50. P(liking math) = $(13 + 9) \div 50 = {}^{11}/_{25}$.

EXAMPLE VENN DIAGRAM

Venn diagram of students who like music and/or math in school. From the diagram, we can see that 13 students like math alone, 9 like both math and music, 24 like music alone, and 4 don't like either.

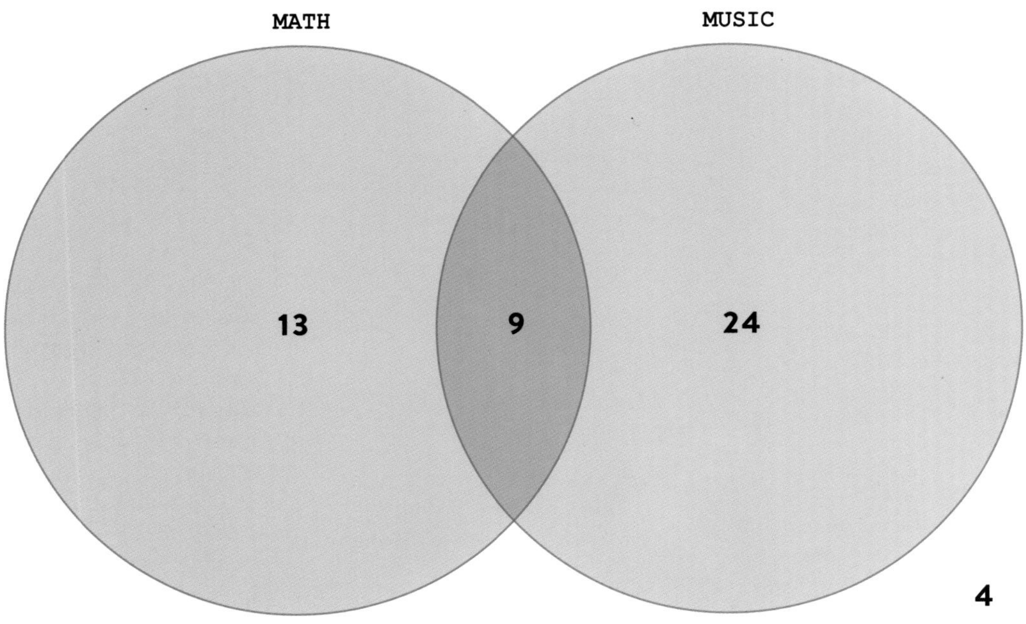

MATH   MUSIC

13   9   24

4

ANSWER THIS

1. Write out the set {square numbers up to 100}.

2. Using the Venn diagram above, calculate the probability that students will like either math or music or both.

STATISTICS AND PROBABILITY

1. Four fair coins are flipped. Calculate the total number of possible outcomes.

a. 16

b. 4

c. 256

d. 12

2. Three six-sided dice are rolled, resulting in 216 possible outcomes. Calculate the probability of only getting odd numbers.

a. 0.5

b. 0.125

c. 0.25

d. 1.0

3. One red ball, two green balls, three orange balls, and four white balls are placed in a box. One ball is removed at random—what is the probability it is not a white ball?

a. 0.4

b. 0.1

c. 0.2

d. 0.6

4. To calculate relative frequencies, Archie rolls a die 20 times and Harry rolls the same die 200 times. Whose results will be more accurate?

a. Archie

b. Harry

5. A coin is flipped 500 times and lands on heads 205 times. What is the relative frequency of getting tails?

a. 1.00

b. 0.50

c. 0.59

d. 0.41

6. If two fair coins are flipped, what is the probability they both show tails?

a. 0.5

b. 0.25

c. 0.75

d. 1.00

7. Complete the tree diagram below:

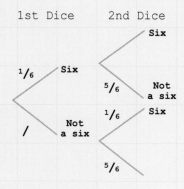

8. A group of 40 teenagers were asked what they did on a Saturday morning: 14 said they played just soccer, 3 played soccer and tennis, 7 played just tennis, and the rest didn't play anything at all. Using this information, fill in the Venn diagram below:

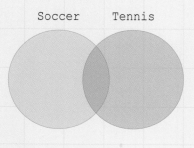

Answers on page 215

SIMPLE SUMMARY

Statistics and probability are used to calculate the chance of something happening. The chance, or probability, of an event happening can range from impossible to certainly occurring.

- The closer to 0 the probability is, the less likely it is; the closer to 1, the more likely it is to happen.

- If there are two activities occurring at the same time, a sample space diagram can be used to help identify all the possible outcomes.

- The probability that any outcome will occur is always 1; therefore, to find the probability that an event doesn't occur is 1 minus the probability it does occur.

- Probability experiments are used to work out relative frequencies and the experimental probability of an outcome occurring, by taking all biases into consideration.

- Use the And rule for calculating when two outcomes both occur; and the Or rule for calculating the probability that either of the two outcomes occur.

- Tree diagrams can be very helpful for working out the probabilities of all the outcomes when you have a combination of events happening one after the other.

- Conditional probabilities are used for dependent events, which are when one outcome affects the probability of the second outcome occurring.

- Venn diagrams are a way of showing sets in circles and squares, and can be used to calculate probability.

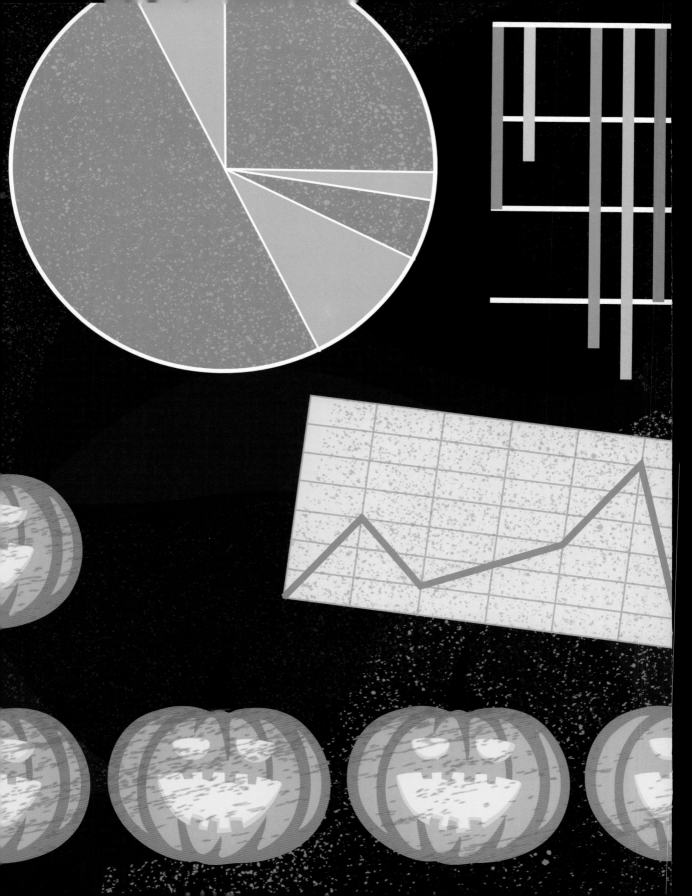

9

GRAPHS: PRESENTING DATA IN THE BEST WAY

Sometimes the best way to present mathematical data is in a graph of some sort. There are many different types of graphs; which one you choose depends on the type of data or correlations you have. This chapter covers seven different ways to present data and also how to calculate the averages: mean, median, and mode.

WHAT YOU WILL LEARN

Presenting data in tables

Schedules and timetables

Bar charts

Pictograms

Scattergraphs

Line graphs

Pie charts

Averages

9.1 PRESENTING DATA IN TABLES

In statistics, lots of information or numerical data is collected. One way to display large amounts of data is in a table. Tables are often easier to read than long lists of information or when the information is written in sentences.

It is important that tables are clearly labeled and set out as logically as possible. The title of a table tells us what information is shown there; the column and row headings indicate what is in each column or row.

For example, there are two people: Christine and Malcolm. Christine gets up at 9:00 a.m., has breakfast at 9:30 a.m., lunch at 12:45 p.m., dinner at 6:50 p.m., and goes to bed at 11:00 p.m. Malcolm, on the other hand, gets up at 7:00 a.m., has breakfast at 7:30 a.m., lunch at 1:45 p.m., dinner at 6:50 p.m., and goes to bed at 10:00 p.m. Those two sentences describe a lot of information, but it is hard to find it quickly. The table below summarizes the information by giving Christine and Malcolm their own columns and listing the activities in the rows.

DAILY SCHEDULES

	CHRISTINE	MALCOLM
Gets up	9:00 a.m.	7:00 a.m.
Eats breakfast	9:30 a.m.	7:30 a.m.
Eats lunch	12:45 p.m.	1:45 p.m.
Eats dinner	6:50 p.m.	6:50 p.m.
Goes to bed	11:00 p.m.	10:00 p.m.

FACT

Tables are often used in sports matches so people can keep track of how their favorite team or player is getting on. In baseball, the number of runs in each inning, hits, errors, outs, balls, and strikes are listed for each team in a table so they are clear to understand.

Now, if we were asked to find out what time Malcolm goes to bed, we would first go to the column with Malcolm at the top, then move down to the row where it says "goes to bed" on the left-hand side. Where that row and column meet is our answer: 10:00 p.m.

Tables can also be useful when counting data or keeping score. In this example, a bunch of friends decided to get involved in the annual butterfly count, counting butterflies in their yard, and they used tally marks to keep score and to calculate the total score:

MADE SIMPLE
KEEPING SCORE

NAME	TALLY	TOTAL SCORE
Zara	卌 卌 卌 II	17
Lehka	卌	5
Nir	II	2
Angeles	卌 卌 IIII	14
Katie	卌 II	7
Karine	IIII	4

To find the total number of different butterflies counted, add up the total scores: 17 + 5 + 2 + 14 + 7 + 4 = 49. If we wanted to see how many more butterflies were in Zara's yard than in Katie's, we would find the difference: 17 - 7 = 10 butterflies.

ANSWER THIS

Fill in the table with the following information transferred into it:

Sarah, Jennifer, and Hannah all have classes in the morning. Sarah has English first at 9:00, then math at 10:00, followed by Spanish at 11:00. Jennifer also has English first, but then goes to art at 10:00 for second and third lessons. Hannah has math first at 9:00, followed by geography, and then Spanish at 11:00. They all have lunch at 12:00.

Morning lessons schedule

	Sarah	Jennifer	Hannah
9:00			
10:00			
11:00			
12:00			

SCHEDULES AND TIMETABLES

Schedules and timetables are used for public transit or school days, and it is useful to be able to read one accurately. You have probably come across schedules and timetables a lot but haven't really thought about the wealth of data they contain.

Timetables are mostly used for public transit, which is where you are most likely going to see them and need to understand their content. When reading a timetable, make sure you know what each column and row stands for—usually there will be names of places or destinations either along the top or down the side, with the corresponding times in the same row or column. In the example bus schedule for downtown Detroit, below, you can see the destinations on the top, and the arrival times for those destinations directly below (in the same column). Each row is the journey of one bus. You can calculate how long it will take to journey between stops by looking at the rows: on the first row, the bus leaves Salina at 9:10 and arrives in Springwells at 9:14, which means that it is a 4-minute bus ride.

FACT

Remember that columns go up and down (like columns that hold up buildings) and rows go side to side (like rowing on water).

MADE SIMPLE
TIMETABLE

Michigan/ Schaefer	Salina	Springwells	Livernois	W Grand Blvd	Trumbull	Rosa Parks Transit Center
9:00	9:10	9:14	9:17	9:22	9:28	9:34
9:30	9:40	9:44	9:47	9:52	9:58	10:04
10:00	10:10	10:14	10:47	10:22	10:28	10:34

Timetable for buses in downtown Detroit, MI. The arrival/departure bus stop names are written across the top, and the times are in the columns below them.

For the example schedule below, Maria is taking the train from New York to meet friends in Boston and her friend Carlos is meeting her on the way. She needs to be in Boston by 6 p.m. and Carlos is joining at Stamford, CT, but is not available until 1 p.m. If you look at the bottom row, at the times the trains arrive in Boston, you can see that the last two trains will not get in on time, so Maria cannot take these. Then look at the Stamford, CT, row and see that only the middle two trains leave after 1 p.m., when Carlos is free, so Maria can take either the 12:30 or the 13:30 train from New York.

TRAIN SCHEDULE

STATION						
New York, NY	10:30	11:30	12:30	13:30	14:30	15:30
New Rochelle, NY	11:00	12:00	13:00	14:00	15:00	16:00
Stamford, CT	11:18	12:18	13:18	14:18	15:18	16:18
New Haven, CT	12:17	13:17	14:17	15:17	16:17	17:17
New London, CT	13:06	14:06	15:06	16:06	17:06	18:06
Providence, RI	14:05	15:05	16:05	17:05	18:05	19:05
Boston, MA	14:58	15:58	16:58	17:58	18:58	19:58

Train schedule for the New York to Boston trip.

ANSWER THIS

Using the bus timetable, left:

1. If Brian gets on the bus at Michigan/Schaefer and his journey takes 28 minutes, where did he get off?
   a. Salina
   b. Springwells
   c. W Grand Blvd
   d. Trumbull

2. How long is the journey between Salina and the Rosa Parks Transit Center?
   a. 4 minutes
   b. 7 minutes
   c. 24 minutes
   d. 30 minutes

Using the New York–Boston train schedule above:

3. If John arrived in Boston, MA, at 16:58, what time did he get the train in New York, NY?
   a. 10:30
   b. 12:30
   c. 14:30
   d. 15:30

4. How long does it take to get from Stamford, CT, to New London, CT?
   a. 1 hour, 36 minutes
   b. 48 minutes
   c. 1 hour
   d. 1 hour, 48 minutes

9.3 BAR CHARTS

Graphs are a way of presenting data that makes comparisons between sets easier to see. Bar charts show a summary of the data and the height of the bars tell you how much of a particular thing you have. They are quite fun to draw (make them as colorful as you like!) and particularly easy to read. It is very important that charts are clearly labeled, including a title that summarizes exactly what you are looking at.

TABLE OF STUDENTS' FAVORITE COLORS	
COLOR	NUMBER OF STUDENTS
RED	4
ORANGE	3
YELLOW	0
GREEN	7
BLUE	10
PURPLE	6

FACT

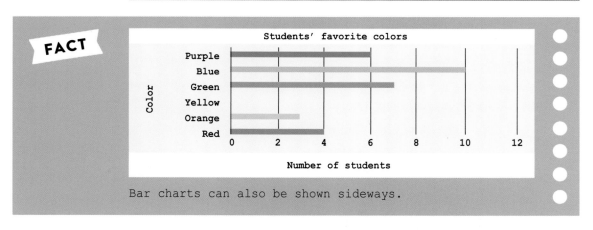

Bar charts can also be shown sideways.

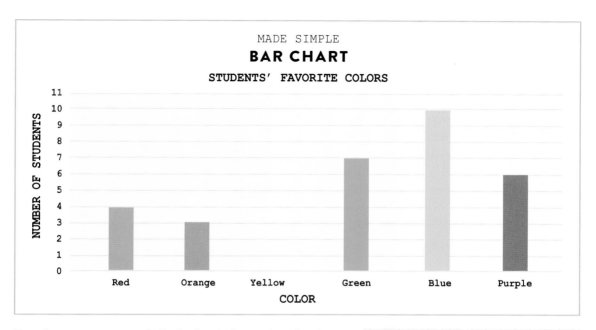

MADE SIMPLE
BAR CHART
STUDENTS' FAVORITE COLORS

Bar charts are a way of displaying information that is easily readable. The table opposite gives confirmation about students' favorite colors. However, in the bar chart above, we can see the same data mapped out, and it is much clearer to see which colors are the favorites. The bottom of the chart contains all the options, such as red, orange, blue, etc., and the left-hand side shows the frequency, or the number of students who chose that color. To find how many students chose blue as their favorite color, look along the bottom until you find "blue" and then look at the bar above it. Look at the height of the bar, follow it horizontally to the axis on the left, and read off the number on that line. So, we can see the height of the blue bar is at 10, which means that 10 students like the color blue the most.

ANSWER THIS

1. How many students chose yellow as their favorite color?
   a. 4
   b. 7
   c. 0
   d. 6

2. Which color was liked by the most students?
   a. Red
   b. Blue
   c. Green
   d. Purple

3. One of the colors was chosen by three students, which color was it?
   a. Orange
   b. Yellow
   c. Purple
   d. Red

9.4 PICTOGRAMS

Pictograms use pictures to represent a specific number of items, for example one picture may be equal to a group of 10 of the same thing. Pictograms require a key, to convey what the pictures mean/how much they represent. They also require knowledge of basic times tables, as you have to identify a suitable factor of all the numbers, which can be broken into halves or quarters, if necessary.

When reading a pictogram, first take note of the key—the box telling you how much a picture is worth. This will be the times table you are going to use, so if a picture is worth 6, then each time the picture is there you multiply by 6 to get the true amount. In the example below, the key states that each dinosaur is equal to 50 dinosaur fossils. To know how many are collected in Australia, for example, there are 2 dinosaurs shown, therefore multiply 2 by 50, indicating 100 dinosaur fossils are found in Australia. In Spain, there are 2½ dinosaurs, so multiply 2.5 by 50 to get the total, 125.

DINOSAUR FOSSILS

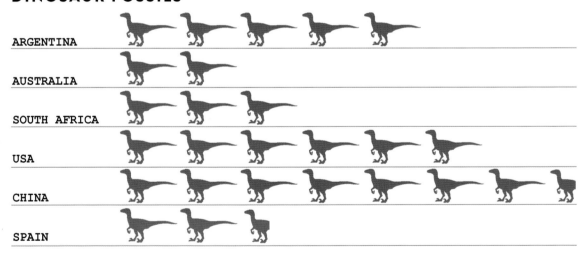

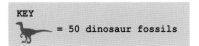

KEY = 50 dinosaur fossils

Pictogram illustrating the number of dinosaur fossils found in various countries around the world.

In pictograms, if a picture is worth 20, then half the picture must be worth half of 20, therefore 10. If there is a quarter of the picture, then it is worth a quarter of 20, which is 5; three-quarters in this case would be equal to 15.

CONVERTING DATA

Year	Number of pumpkins
2015	30
2016	45
2017	60
2018	50
2019	55

Key: = 10 pumpkins

Data and corresponding pictogram illustrating the number of pumpkins seen each year.

To convert data to a pictogram, first choose an appropriate image and a key, to show how much one picture or image is worth. It is best to choose a number that goes easily into the data you have for the key. For example, on Halloween, some houses put out carved pumpkins; in some years there are more pumpkins than others, so David decided to count out how many he could see each year. Using a pumpkin as the picture, each pumpkin is worth 10 "real" pumpkins (any less and there will be a lot of pumpkins in the pictogram!). In 2016, there were 45 pumpkins, which is not a multiple of 10, but half the image can be used to represent 5 pumpkins.

ANSWER THIS

Using the dinosaur fossils pictogram, answer the following questions:

1. How many dinosaur fossils were found in the USA?
   a. 6
   b. 300
   c. 60
   d. 120

2. How many dinosaur fossils were found in China?
   a. 375
   b. 300
   c. 7.5
   d. 75

3. 200 dinosaur fossils were found in Canada; how would this be drawn on the pictogram?

Using the pumpkin pictogram, answer the following question:

4. How many pumpkins were seen in 2019?
   a. 550
   b. 5.5
   c. 55
   d. 5

9.5 SCATTERGRAPHS

Scattergraphs are used to see if there is a link or a relationship between two things, also known as variables. A scattergraph will show if two things are closely related, weakly related, or not related at all. If two variables are related, they are correlated. If two variables are correlated, you should be able to draw a straight line through, or close to, the majority of points on the graph.

There are three types of correlation: positive, negative, and none. A positive correlation is when one variable increases, so too does the other variable. In a negative correlation, when one variable increases, the other decreases, and if there is no correlation, there will just be a random mess of points across the graph, i.e. the increase of one variable has no relationship to the other variable.

FACT

Correlation does not mean causation. Just because two things are correlated does not mean that one affects the other. For example, the divorce rate in Maine closely correlates with the amount of margarine consumed in the USA; however, one does not cause or affect the other, otherwise margarine would be the cause of all the divorces!

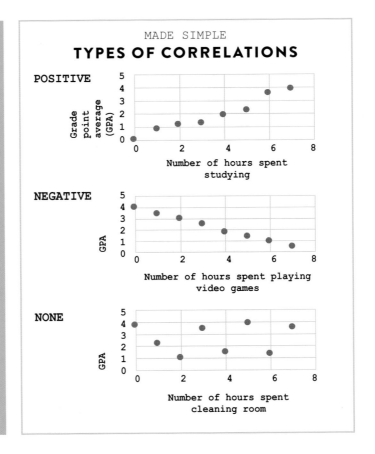

MADE SIMPLE
TYPES OF CORRELATIONS

Additionally, there are weak and/or strong correlations. If the points make a fairly straight line, then the variables are strongly correlated. If the points don't line up as nicely but there is a correlation, it's called a weak correlation. The strength of the correlation depends on how many and how close the points are to making a line.

For example, look at the relationship between temperature each day and the number of people at the lake. As shown in the graph, as the temperature increases, the number of people increases; therefore, there is a positive correlation. As the points are close to making a straight line, there is a strong positive correlation. This means that as the days are warmer, there are more people going to the beach, which makes sense.

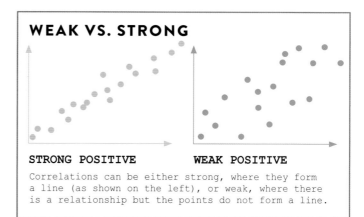

WEAK VS. STRONG

STRONG POSITIVE   WEAK POSITIVE

Correlations can be either strong, where they form a line (as shown on the left), or weak, where there is a relationship but the points do not form a line.

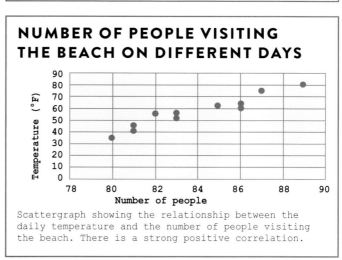

NUMBER OF PEOPLE VISITING THE BEACH ON DIFFERENT DAYS

Scattergraph showing the relationship between the daily temperature and the number of people visiting the beach. There is a strong positive correlation.

ANSWER THIS

1. When one variable increases, and the other variable also increases, what kind of correlation is this?
   a. Positive
   b. Negative
   c. None

2. The scattergraph right shows what kind of relationship?
   a. Positive
   b. Negative
   c. None

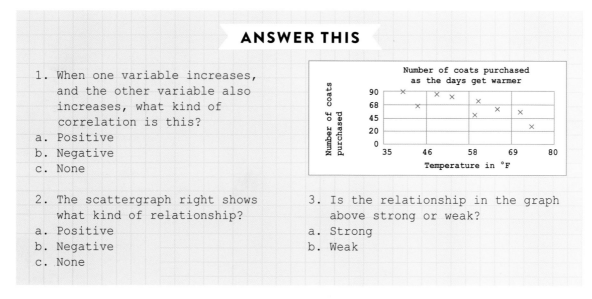

3. Is the relationship in the graph above strong or weak?
   a. Strong
   b. Weak

9.6 LINE GRAPHS

Line graphs use lines instead of bars to show data. The graph can either show a smooth line or have points joined up by lines. The line goes where the top of the bars from a bar chart would go, so it's read in the same way. This type of graph is an effective way of illustrating how things might change over time or distance.

Line graphs are a clear way of showing if something is greater or lesser than the point before it and if there are any trends. Additionally, they are used to compare two sets of data. For example, Rose wants to compare how the monthly temperature in two cities—Kansas City and Saint Paul, Minnesota—changes over the course of a year. Once she has the information, Rose uses a line graph to

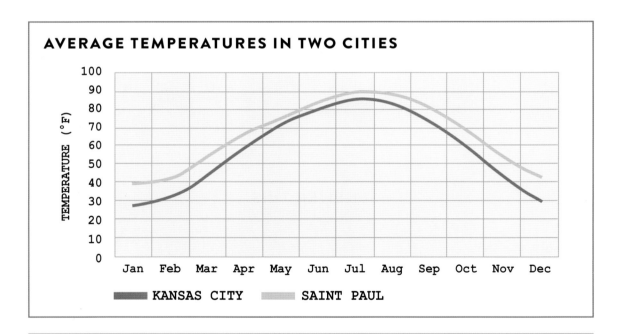

AVERAGE TEMPERATURES IN TWO CITIES

KANSAS CITY   SAINT PAUL

FACT Usually when people are talking about graphs, they mean line graphs, as these are the most common types of graphs used and can be applied in a lot of different circumstances.

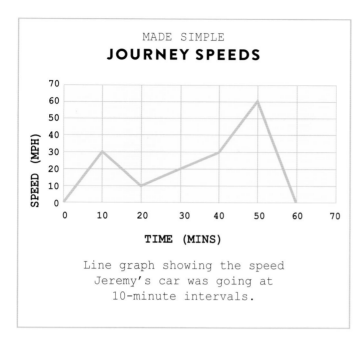

MADE SIMPLE
JOURNEY SPEEDS

SPEED (MPH)

TIME (MINS)

Line graph showing the speed
Jeremy's car was going at
10-minute intervals.

show the information more effectively, and this is seen in the illustration opposite. Rose can clearly see that the temperatures in June are very similar but Kansas City is much warmer than Saint Paul for the rest of the year.

Key points

Sometimes it is not a smooth line through the points, and so it's better to show the points joined up one by one. For example, Jeremy's journey to his grandparents' house takes around an hour and the car travels through the suburbs, town center, and then rural roads, and so travels at different speeds. Jeremy notes down the speed every 10 minutes and plots it on a line graph, shown in the illustration above. Joining up the points shows how Jeremy's journey changes over time, and where he was traveling the fastest, or slowing down as he was going into the town center, for instance. Line graphs where the points are joined up like this are best for showing key points on journeys.

**Using the temperature
line graph:**

1. In February, which city has the higher average maximum temperature?
a. Kansas City
b. Saint Paul

2. In which month did Saint Paul's maximum temperature never dip below 60°F?
a. March
b. September
c. November
d. January

**Using the journey speeds
line graph:**

3. How many minutes into the journey were they traveling at 60 mph?
a. 10 minutes
b. 30 minutes
c. 50 minutes
d. 60 minutes

4. 30 minutes into the journey, Jeremy left the town center and was able to pick up speed, how fast was he going then?
a. 20 mph
b. 30 mph
c. 40 mph
d. 50 mph

9.7 PIE CHARTS

Pie charts are used to show proportions of a total. They look like a pie that is divided into slices, the size of the slice directly corresponding to a proportion of the total. In all pie charts, the fractions must add to 1, or, if using percentages, they must add up to 100.

To read a pie chart, you have to judge how much of the total is taken up by each specific color (unless the exact amounts are provided). For example, it's the first week of the summer vacation and Beth spends her time sleeping, playing video games, playing outside, eating, and reading. She spends different amounts of time on each activity within the day, as presented in the bar chart below. We can see that the section for sleeping makes up nearly half of the pie, which means she spent around half her time sleeping. The orange section covers a quarter of the pie, so Beth spends around a quarter of her time playing video games. The smallest section is reading, so she spends very little time overall reading.

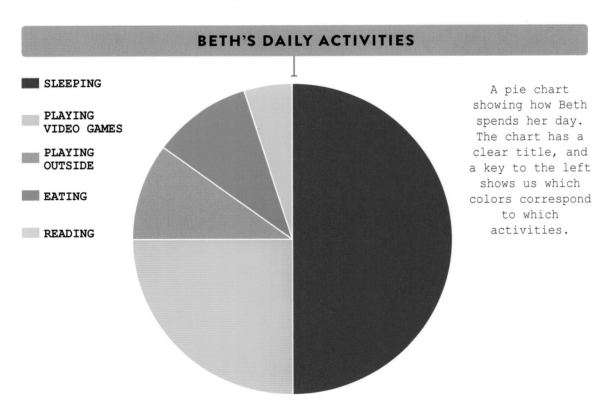

BETH'S DAILY ACTIVITIES

- SLEEPING
- PLAYING VIDEO GAMES
- PLAYING OUTSIDE
- EATING
- READING

A pie chart showing how Beth spends her day. The chart has a clear title, and a key to the left shows us which colors correspond to which activities.

Estimating segment values

If we know how much the total pie is worth, we can estimate how much each section is, rather than just using a fraction or percentage. In this example, Rishi is redecorating her bedroom and spends $2,000. She bought new furniture, paint, flooring, bedding, accessories, and curtains. The pie chart shows how much of the total Rishi spent on each item. The key shows that the orange section relates to how much Rishi spent on furniture, which covers around half of the pie; therefore, Rishi spent about half of the $2,000 on furniture, around $1,000. Remember, this is an estimate.

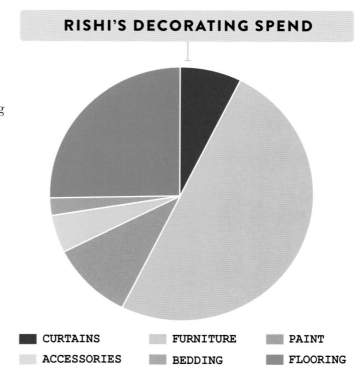

RISHI'S DECORATING SPEND

- CURTAINS
- FURNITURE
- PAINT
- ACCESSORIES
- BEDDING
- FLOORING

A pie chart illustrating how much of the total $2,000 Rishi spends on each item when redecorating her room.

ANSWER THIS

1. As there are 24 hours in a day, calculate roughly how long Beth spends playing video games (using the first pie chart)?
a. 6 hours
b. 10 hours
c. 12 hours
d. 4 hours

2. Beth spends as much time playing outside as one other activity. Which is it?
a. Sleeping
b. Playing video games
c. Eating
d. Reading

3. The green section in the Rishi's redecorating spend pie chart covers roughly one quarter of the pie. How much money does that mean she spent on flooring?
a. $2,000
b. $500
c. $400
d. $1,000

4. What did Rishi spend the least on?
a. Curtains
b. Paint
c. Accessories
d. Bedding

AVERAGES: MEDIAN, MODE, MEAN

An average is a number that summarizes data and can help with comparisons of other groups of data. People often refer to mean when they talk about an average; however, there are three types of averages—median, mode, and mean—each affected by different things and appropriate in specific circumstances. The median and mode are relatively simple to identify, but you need to perform calculations to find the mean.

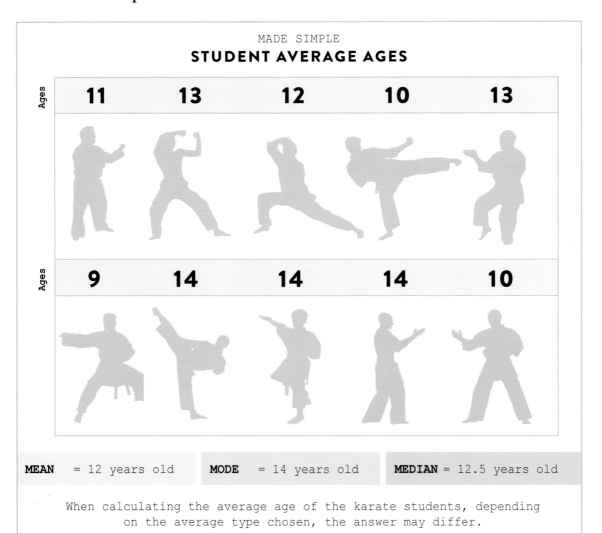

MADE SIMPLE
STUDENT AVERAGE AGES

| Ages | 11 | 13 | 12 | 10 | 13 |

| Ages | 9 | 14 | 14 | 14 | 10 |

MEAN = 12 years old   **MODE** = 14 years old   **MEDIAN** = 12.5 years old

When calculating the average age of the karate students, depending on the average type chosen, the answer may differ.

MEAN EQUATION

$$\text{MEAN} = \frac{\text{Sum of all numbers}}{\text{How many numbers there are}}$$

Median

The median is the middle number when all the data is ranked in ascending order (lowest to highest). You must remember to rank the data and not just pick the number in the middle of the list. If the middle ends up being between two numbers, you take the halfway point between them. For example, an instructor is trying to figure out the median ages of kids in his karate class. The ages of the students in the class are: 11, 13, 12, 10, 13, 9, 14, 14, 14, 10. First, put the ages in order: 9, 10, 10, 11, 12, 13, 13, 14, 14, 14. As there are 10 numbers, the halfway point is between the fifth and sixth numbers: between 12 and 13, which is 12.5. Therefore, the median age is 12.5.

Mode

The mode is the most common data value, the one that's repeated the most. If there are a lot of numbers in the data, it is recommended to create a tally table, to check you are counting all the points (this goes for the median as well). In the example above, there are two students aged 10, and two students aged 13, but there are three students aged 14. The mode student age would be 14 years old.

Mean

The mean is the total of the numbers divided by the number of numbers. When trying to find the mean of the students' ages above, first add all the ages together to get the total: 11 + 13 + 12 + 10 + 13 + 9 + 14 + 14 + 14 + 10 = 120. Next, divide this total by the number of ages (10 students): 120 ÷ 10 = 12. The mean age for the karate class students is 12.

FACT

To remember which measure is which: MEDian is the MIDdle value; MOde is MOst common; and MEAN is the MEANest, as you have to do a lot to work it out.

●●●●●●●●

ANSWER THIS

1. The temperature was taken every day for 15 days (in °F):
   64, 64, 67, 64, 69, 64, 65, 65, 63, 67, 63, 64, 65, 68, 65.
a. Rank the temperatures in ascending order.
b. Find the median temperature.
c. Find the mode temperature.
d. Calculate the mean temperature.

GRAPHS

1. Here is a table of the morning train journeys from Union Station in Denver, CO, to Denver Airport Station:

Union Station	38th & Blake St.	40th & Colorado Blvd.	Central Park Station	Peoria Station	40th Avenue	61st & Pena Blvd.	Denver Airport Station
7:30	7:34	7:39	7:43	7:46	7:52	7:55	8:07
7:45	7:49	7:54	7:58	8:01	8:07	8:10	8:22
8:00	8:04	8:09	8:13	8:16	8:22	8:25	8:37
8:15	8:19	8:24	8:28	8:31	8:37	8:40	8:52

i. How long does the train take from Union Station to 61st & Pena Blvd.?

ii. If Paul gets on the train at 40th & Colorado Blvd. at 8:09, what time will he arrive at Denver Airport Station?

2. Using an apple icon, fill in the following information:
On Monday, 16 apples were sold; 12 were sold on Tuesday; 4 sold on Wednesday; 10 on Thursday; 24 on Friday. Monday has been done for you.

Key 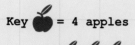 = 4 apples

Monday 🍎🍎🍎🍎

Tuesday

Wednesday

Thursday

Friday

3. Tracey has collected daily temperature readings for a year in three cities, and she wants to present them in a graph to show how the temperature in each city rises and falls throughout the year. Which is the most appropriate type of graph?

a. Pie chart

b. Pictogram

c. Line graph

d. Bar chart

4. A litter of 10 kittens is born, weighing the following (in ounces): 4, 4, 3, 9, 5, 7, 4, 8, 5, 9.

i. Calculate the mode kitten weight.

ii. Calculate the median kitten weight.

iii. Calculate the mean kitten weight.

Answers on page 216

SIMPLE SUMMARY

Sometimes the best way to present mathematical data is in a graph of some sort. There are many different types of graphs, which one you choose depends on the type of data or correlations you have.

- Tables are often easier to read than long lists of information or when the information is written in sentences.

- When reading a timetable, make sure you know what each column and row stands for.

- Bar charts show a summary of the data and the height of the bars tell you how much of a particular thing you have.

- Pictograms are charts that use pictures to represent a specific number of items.

- A scattergraph will show if two things are closely related, weakly related, or not related at all.

- There are three types of correlation: positive, negative, and none.

- Line graphs are a clear way of showing if something is greater or lesser than the point before it and if there are any trends, and they are used to compare two sets of data.

- To read a pie chart, you have to judge how much of the total is taken up by each specific color (unless the exact amounts are provided).

- There are three types of averages—median, mode, and mean—each affected by different things and appropriate in specific circumstances.

10
ORIGINS AND USE OF MATH

Math does not just exist as a subject in schools—it forms the basis of understanding the world around us. The history of math as we understand it today comes from all around the globe and is universal. This chapter covers both the early history of math and how it is used today in various ways.

WHAT YOU WILL LEARN

History of early mathematics

Math in modern life

Problem-solving skills

Universal language

Symbols and concepts

Math in computing, science, and nature

HISTORY OF EARLY MATHEMATICS

From early counting in prehistoric times, to ancient civilizations moving away from magic toward logic, the math we see and use today has had a long history of being discovered and refined. We take modern math for granted, but there was a time when zeros weren't used in calculations and there weren't any easy-to-use formulas to calculate areas and volumes.

The first instances of math used by humans was counting and tallying marks left on bones, such as the Lebombo bone found in Africa from more than 30,000 years ago. The Ishango bone (around 20,000 years old) has notches carved into it in columns, which indicates an understanding of addition. With the development of civilizations, more complex math—such as working out areas or shapes of land, or calculating taxes—were necessary.

LEBOMBO BONE

Carved notches

Some ancient bones were found to contain carved notches, indicating people were using tallies to count, and may even have understood prime numbers.

The Sumerians (from modern-day Iraq) developed ways of grouping numbers or objects to make the description of larger numbers easier. They used a base 60 (sexagesimal) system which led to the modern-day times: 60 seconds to a minute, 60 minutes to an hour. The Ancient Egyptians then introduced the base 10 number system (around 3000 BC).

FACT   The number zero was previously used as a placeholder and not as a number in its own right. Brahmagupta, an Indian mathematician, established rules for dealing with the number zero in the seventh century.

Early pioneers

Ancient Greek mathematics was focused on geometry. The most famous Greek mathematician is Pythagoras, whose theorem on right-angled triangles is still used and taught today, despite being described as far back as 500 BC. Pythagoras, Theano (the first notable mathematician who was a woman), Plato, and Aristotle all contributed to the idea of proof: that is, the deductive method of using reason and logic to prove or disprove ideas and theorems. This is when magic gave way to numbers and logical reasoning.

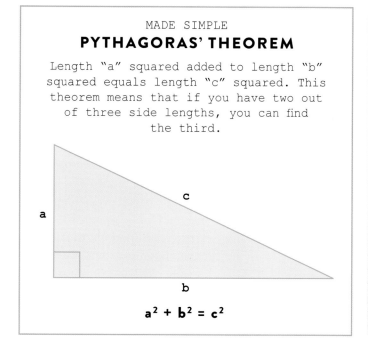

MADE SIMPLE
PYTHAGORAS' THEOREM

Length "a" squared added to length "b" squared equals length "c" squared. This theorem means that if you have two out of three side lengths, you can find the third.

$$a^2 + b^2 = c^2$$

For a few hundred years following the fall of various civilizations, not much progress was achieved. Jumping forward to the eighth century AD, the Islamic Empire used complex geometric patterns in building decorations, raising mathematics to the level where it was considered art. They discovered all the different forms of symmetry that can be drawn on a 2-D surface. Al-Khwarizmi, a famous Islamic mathematician, developed the method of balancing algebra equations, which led to the mathematical language used today.

10.2 MATH IN MODERN LIFE

Mathematics is everywhere. In the modern world, math is both relevant and crucial to everyday life, which is interesting, as it is usually one of the least favorite subjects at school. In particular, math is useful for basic calculations, telling the time, budgeting and finance, cooking, and general problem-solving.

The most obvious and crucial way we use math is basic arithmetic. Throughout the day, we may need to do basic calculations, such as adding or subtracting, and we usually don't give a second thought to it, but it is math, and we learned it as children. It is a learned and very useful skill, especially to be able to do it in our heads, quickly.

Math can help with money and finances. As we saw in earlier chapters, you need to be able to understand and use percentages, decimal numbers, and fractions when dealing with money or budgeting, to add up everything you have paid for or minus taxes, for example. Additionally, the ability to calculate interest will help with deciding where best to put money or whether an investment is worth it. Bank accounts often offer varying interest rates and bonuses for savings accounts, so it is helpful to be able to understand these.

You will find that math is used in a multitude of ways throughout your day, if you are paying attention!

FACT   Imagine a world without numbers. How do you think you would communicate amounts, time, proportions, or measurements? Numbers and calculations are used in almost every part of our lives.

1. What topic in math do you need to understand when dealing with finances?
   a. 3-D shapes
   b. Percentages
   c. Nets
   d. Tree diagrams

2. What is the most used type of math in everyday life?
   a. Simplifying terms
   b. Factorizing
   c. Basic arithmetic
   d. Patterns and sequences

Time to learn

Math also helps you tell the time. Prior to learning it in class, very few people would be able to tell the time, or understand the fractions of an hour, etc. How many times a day do you look at the clock, or how many times do you calculate if you have enough time to get something done, i.e., brush your teeth before school, or catch the 8:30 a.m. bus? Your day is structured by time.

Baking and cooking both utilize your math skills. Knowing how to convert between metric and imperial units can help with international recipes, or using ratios to increase or decrease the ingredients in line with the amount you are making.

MADE SIMPLE
CONVERTING INGREDIENTS

Recipe for 10 cookies
Converted amounts

	(metric)	(imperial)
Eggs	1	1
Flour	250 g	8.8 oz
Sugar	200 g	7 oz
Butter	100 g	3.5 oz

Math helps us convert measures so we can use international recipes.

LESSON 10.3 PROBLEM-SOLVING SKILLS

Students often ask, "What is the point in doing math?" Practicing and learning mathematics helps improve our ability to analyze problems. Being able to think critically and analyze a problem is a key skill in life—and often in jobs. This leads to reasoning skills, which are useful to help solve problems and identify solutions.

MADE SIMPLE
DAILY DECISIONS

WILL I MAKE IT?

Daisy

How fast?

How far?

Just crossing the road is an example of problem solving, as you need to evaluate car speed and crossing distance to decide whether you can make it to the other side safely.

One of the key skills you learn in math is to work systematically. In other words, you learn to identify the problem and the relevant information, and then work through it, step by step. For example, practicing BIDMAS or PEMDAS helps you learn to identify which parts of the problem you have to solve first, rather than just launching yourself at the problem. Working systematically decreases the chance of mistakes.

Just going about daily life, we encounter potential problems that require us to analyze data and make a conclusion. For example, when Daisy wants to cross a road, she has to work out roughly how quickly the traffic is traveling, if any; the distance she needs to cross; and how long it may take her. She is most likely not carrying out exact calculations in her head, but rather she is making estimates as to how likely she will be able to cross and not get run over by a car, thus solving the problem.

The RIDE method is widely used for problem solving: R—read the problem correctly; I—identify the relevant information (underline it); D—determine the operation/calculations and unit for the answer; E—enter the correct terms and calculate.

Problem-solving skills are not necessarily about carrying out calculations with numbers; they are more about making an estimate of a likelihood or amount. Another example of solving a problem is working out whether you need to wear a coat when you go out. The daily weather forecast often provides a chance of rain—without understanding probability and chance, you would not be able to figure out if you need to take a coat or not when you go out. This is a relatively simple example, but demonstrates how being able to use information effectively (therefore solving potential problems) helps in your daily life.

EVALUATING

80%

Practicing and learning math helps identify useful information: even though it is not currently raining, there is a high probability it may at some point, and so it's best to take an umbrella.

ANSWER THIS

Practice your problem-solving skills with these questions:

1. A rocket is traveling to Mars—which piece of information will not be useful to the astronauts?
a. Distance
b. Speed
c. Angle or trajectory
d. The weather on the planet Jupiter

2. The weather forecast states there is a 90% chance of rain. You don't have a coat, so should you take an umbrella when you go out?
a. Yes, take an umbrella
b. No, don't take an umbrella

3. Julia has 1 hour before she needs to leave. She still needs to: have breakfast, which takes around 30 minutes; brush her teeth, which takes 5 minutes; do her hair, which takes 10 minutes; and get changed, which takes about 20 minutes. Does she have enough time?
a. Yes
b. No

10.4 UNIVERSAL LANGUAGE

Math is a language, as it uses a specific vocabulary and grammar to communicate concepts. It is the same all over the world; therefore, it can act as a universal language. In a universal language, a phrase or formula will stay the same and have the same meaning, no matter what other language is around it.

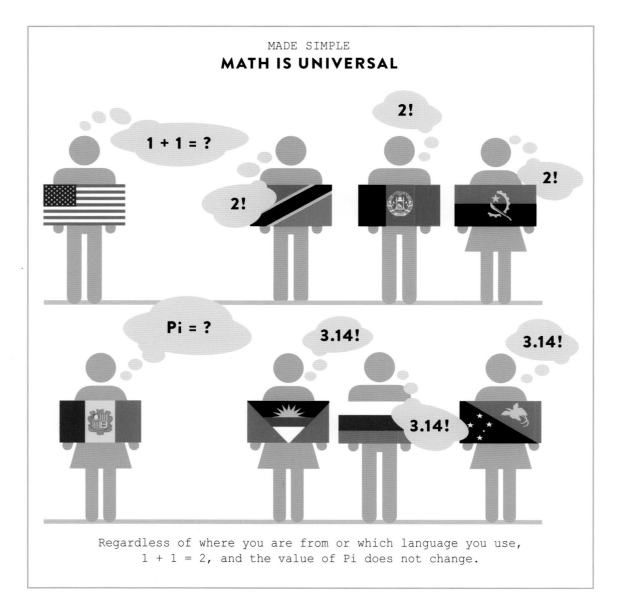

MADE SIMPLE

MATH IS UNIVERSAL

Regardless of where you are from or which language you use,
1 + 1 = 2, and the value of Pi does not change.

You may have never heard mathematics be referred to as a language before, but it is. Language is a collection of words, codes, or characters used to communicate processes. Math uses symbols that have meaning and employs grammar rules that outline how the characters are used, e.g., division ($\div$) means to see how many times a number goes into another number. Math contains specific nouns: numerals, fractions, expressions, formulas, pi; and verbs with specific meanings: division, multiplication, square, addition, etc.

International appeal

There is also a set of international rules that people carrying out mathematics abide by, which is something individual languages do not necessarily have. Formulas are always read left to right, and calculations must be carried out according to BODMAS, BIDMAS or PEMDAS (see page 38). The Latin alphabet is used for variables such as x or y, and the Greek alphabet is used for specific concepts such as Pi (π).

Math is the only language shared across the ages, regardless of culture, history, or religion. $1 + 1$ will always equal 2, and Pi is approximately 3.14—this will not change, no matter where you are. Every civilization in history has math in common, and while numbers and symbols may change, the principals and concepts remain the same across time. Despite all our differences as humans, math is the common language that we all share.

ANSWER THIS

1. Which is a used noun in math?
   a. Multiplying
   b. Numeral
   c. Dividing
   d. Subtracting

2. Which alphabet is used for variables?
   a. Greek
   b. Latin

3. What is the value of Pi (to two decimal places)?
   a. 1
   b. 3
   c. 3.09
   d. 3.14

4. In which direction are formulas read?
   a. Left to right
   b. Right to left

SYMBOLS AND CONCEPTS

Mathematics has a particular set of symbols and terms that communicate specific meanings. Students, and generally people existing in the modern world, should know or being able to recognize a lot of these symbols or terms. Additionally, math is subdivided into key branches, and it is important to be able to understand how each branch is dedicated to particular types of math.

Mathematics is often described by its branches: algebra, geometry, probability and statistics, and ratio and proportion. It is important to understand the difference between these branches. Algebra is math that uses letters and symbols to represent numbers in formulas and expressions. Geometry is the section in math that studies shapes, size, positions, angles, and dimensions. Probability is the study of how likely events are to occur. Statistics is the practice of collecting and analyzing numerical data to see if there are relationships. Ratio, in math, is the comparison of two sizes, whereas proportion refers to the equality of two ratios. As stated before, it also has a series of symbols with specific meanings. Those shown in the table opposite are useful for most math.

ANSWER THIS

1. Which is not a branch of mathematics:
   a. French
   b. Geometry
   c. Algebra
   d. Statistics

2. Algebra uses what instead of numbers?
   a. Letters
   b. Ones and zeros
   c. Degrees
   d. +

3. Which is the symbol for a square root?
   a. +
   b. √
   c. ()
   d. ÷

4. What is the symbol > known as?
   a. Less than
   b. Percentage
   c. More than
   d. Equals

MAIN MATH SYMBOLS

SYMBOL		MEANING
+		Addition or plus
—		Subtraction or minus
×	*****	Multiplication
÷	**/**	Division
=		Equals
<		Less than
>		More than
°		Degrees (either in angles or Fahrenheit/Centigrade)
√		Square root
2		Power
.		Decimal point
,		Thousands and millions separator
( )		Brackets
%		Percentages

The table above shows all the main symbols used in everyday math that you need to be able to recognize, understand, and use.

LESSON
10.6 MATH IN COMPUTING

From the original analytical machine engineered by Charles Babbage in the nineteenth century to compute times tables, to Ada Lovelace's early computer program, math has always been at the core of computing. Early computers used binary systems—which use only zeros and ones as a code for numbers, words, or actions—and would only perform simple tasks. Today's computers are used to carry out calculations at breakneck speed—something people would take years to do themselves.

BINARY AND HEXADECIMAL

Decimal numbers	Binary code	Hexadecimal code
0	0	0
1	1	1
2	10	2
3	11	3
4	100	4
5	101	5
6	110	6
7	111	7
8	1000	8
9	1001	9
10	1010	A
11	1011	B
12	1100	C
13	1101	D
14	1110	E
15	1111	F

Binary code and hexadecimal code for numbers 0 to 15, as used in computing.

A "computer" used to be the name given to someone who performed calculations, until mechanical versions were invented and computer "code" was written. Binary math formed the basis of these new computers, and, in fact, is the core of how a computer operates. Binary numbers are made up of only zeros and ones—no other numbers are used. As computers developed, they started to use a hexadecimal system: a combination of numbers 0 to 9 and letters A to F which allowed for more complex language and calculations. These binary or hexadecimal languages form instructions, called code, telling the computer what to do. Nowadays, more complex coding language is used, but the code is still run using mathematical instructions. Modern computing allows us to calculate complex concepts much more quickly than if we did it by hand.

HTML CODING

```html
<html lang="en">

<head>

  <meta charset="utf-8">


    <title>Math Made Simple</title>

    <meta name="description"
    content="Math Made Simple">

    <meta name="author"
    content="SitePoint">


    <link rel="stylesheet" href="css/
    styles.css?v=1.0">


</head>


<body>

  <script src="js/scripts.js"></
script>

</body>

</html>
```

Binary coding has given way to complex coding with words and symbols, based on mathematical principles, such as the basic HTML template code, above, for a website.

ANSWER THIS

1. What numbers are used in binary systems?

2. How is 15 written in binary?

3. How is 11 written in the hexadecimal system?

10.7 MATH IN SCIENCE

Knowledge of mathematics is essential in science, and forms the basis for how ideas and concepts are either discovered or described. Statistics are often used in biology, while equations and algebra are widely used in chemistry and physics. Scientific theories are often written as formulas, and basic arithmetic is used to collect and store data about the world around us.

MADE SIMPLE
APPLIED MATH

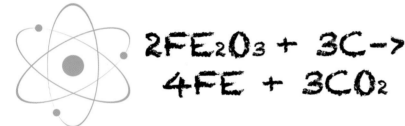

$$2FE_2O_3 + 3C \rightarrow 4FE + 3CO_2$$

Math is used extensively in the three sciences: in physics, measurements are used for the very big and the very small things in our universe; in chemistry, balancing equations are used in chemical experiments; and in biology, statistics are used to test hypotheses.

Physics

The application of mathematics in order to understand the laws of the world and the universe is known as physics. Most subjects in physics use mathematics. Math is used to produce formulas, so we can describe established theories and concepts. In addition, when looking at atoms or distances in space, standard form is used widely. Furthermore, measurements are used in physics to describe the weight of an atom (μg) or star (tons).

Chemistry

The study of chemicals is chemistry, which looks at what chemicals are made of, what they can do, and how we can combine them to make new ones. Chemical equations (written as formulas) describe the chemical

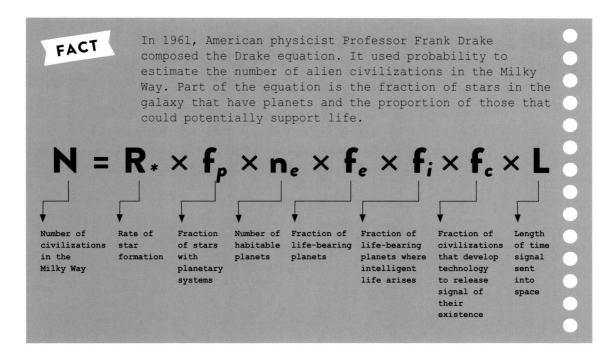

In 1961, American physicist Professor Frank Drake composed the Drake equation. It used probability to estimate the number of alien civilizations in the Milky Way. Part of the equation is the fraction of stars in the galaxy that have planets and the proportion of those that could potentially support life.

$$N = R_* \times f_p \times n_e \times f_e \times f_i \times f_c \times L$$

Number of civilizations in the Milky Way

Rate of star formation

Fraction of stars with planetary systems

Number of habitable planets

Fraction of life-bearing planets

Fraction of life-bearing planets where intelligent life arises

Fraction of civilizations that develop technology to release signal of their existence

Length of time signal sent into space

reactions, or changes, when substances are combined. Within these chemical reactions, the ratio of chemicals is important, as are the proportions or fractions of chemicals used. Basic arithmetic is used in balancing equations, to make sure the correct number or amount of a substance is made.

Biology

In biology, the study of living organisms, statistics is widely used. Biological sciences are often focused on the relationship between two things or variables. For example, a biological experiment could look at the correlation between sunshine and the rate of photosynthesis. To do this, scientists must know how to use standard measurement units, and accurately collect and analyze the data. This branch of math is known as statistics. In addition, scientists have to appropriately present the data and, as we saw in Chapter 8, there are lots of different ways in which to do that.

ANSWER THIS

1. Which scientific subject can be described as the application of mathematics in order to understand the laws of the universe?

2. Chemical reactions are written using which type of mathematics?

3. Which branch of mathematics is used widely in biology?

10.8 MATH IN NATURE

Math is used to describe lots of things in nature, such as the height of a tree and its yearly growth rate. Math is also often used to explain natural patterns found in the world around us. Early mathematicians tried to explain order in nature by looking to patterns—many of which have been discovered. Here we will discuss the main four: symmetry, fractals, spirals, and tessellations.

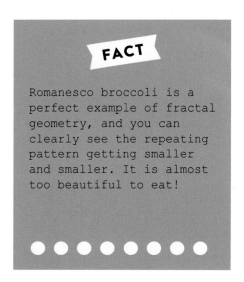

FACT

Romanesco broccoli is a perfect example of fractal geometry, and you can clearly see the repeating pattern getting smaller and smaller. It is almost too beautiful to eat!

MADE SIMPLE
NATURAL PATTERNS

The starfish (top left) is an example of bilateral symmetry: if you cut it down the middle, you would have two mirroring halves. Shells (top right) often show fractal patterns when opened, as they have the same repeated shape in different sizes. Bottom left shows the spiral pattern as seen in hurricanes, tornadoes, and typhoons. Beehives (bottom right) are a prime example of a tessellating pattern, one shape that repeats over and over.

Symmetry is everywhere in nature; all you have to do is look at the average human body to see that it is symmetrical. In nature, there is radial and bilateral symmetry. Bilateral symmetry means an organism has two mirroring halves (both sides reflect the same shape). This is seen in humans, insects, birds, mammals, spiders, etc., and is the most common form of symmetry. Radial symmetry means that a shape (usually a cone or circular shape) is symmetrical around a central point. This is seen in jellyfish, some flowers, and sea anemones.

Fractals as described by the mathematician Benoit B. Mandelbrot 40 years ago, are patterns that are repeated at different scales. Trees are a good example of fractals, from the network of veins in a leaf all the way up to the forking branches, they are repeating units at different sizes or scales. Snowflakes are particularly beautiful representations of fractals.

Spirals are also seen in nature. Hurricanes, tornadoes, and typhoons are spiral in nature, as are galaxies. It seems to be a very common growth pattern, and it has been argued by scientists that it is the most efficient way for an organism to grow. The mathematician Fibonacci tried to understand order in nature and studied spiral patterns in plants. Plants such as the aloe plant grow in a spiral pattern.

Tessellations are patterns that contain repeating units or shapes; however, they are different from fractals as the repeating units are the same size. Bees' honeycomb is a well-known example of tessellation, where the six-sided cells are repeated to create a complex pattern. The repeated diamond-shape scales on a snake are another example.

ORIGINS AND USE OF MATH

1. The first instance of humans counting was marks carved onto bones. What kind of marks were these?

   a. Latin letters

   b. Tally marks

   c. Greek letters

   d. Modern numbers

2. Which group introduced the base 10 number system?

   a. Cave people

   b. Ancient Greeks

   c. Ancient Egyptians

   d. Modern humans

3. Math is important in problem solving. Try to apply that skill to this question: Meg is planning a car journey, which of the following does she not need to take into consideration?

   a. Amount of gas in the car

   b. The size of her television

   c. Roadworks on the way

   d. Distance she has to drive

4. Joe and three friends are making cakes for a charity fair. They can each make two cakes every hour, and have three hours to make all the cakes. They need to make 30 cakes, do they have enough people to do it?

   a. Yes

   b. No

5. Math is a universal language. That means:

   a. Principles stay the same regardless of other languages around it.

   b. Principles change with other languages around it.

6. Which branch of mathematics uses letters in place of numbers?

   a. Geometry

   b. Ratio

   c. Algebra

   d. Probability

7. Sometimes "/" is used as a symbol for which calculation?

   a. Addition

   b. Division

   c. Multiplication

   d. Subtraction

8. What is the name of the number system or code that contains ones and zeros and nothing else?

   a. Decimal

   b. Sexadecimal

   c. Hexadecimal

   d. Binary

9. Identify the patterns found in the following images:

   a. Beehive:

   b. Spiderweb:

Answers on page 217

SIMPLE SUMMARY

Math forms the basis of understanding the world around us. The history of math as we understand it today comes from all around the globe and is universal.

- The first instances of math used by humans was counting and tallying marks left on bones, such as the Lebombo bone found in Africa from more than 30,000 years ago.

- Most of Greek mathematics was focused on geometry.

- Math is useful for basic calculations, telling the time, budgeting and finance, cooking, and general problem-solving.

- Problem-solving skills are not necessarily about carrying out calculations with numbers; they are more about making an estimate of a likelihood or amount.

- Math helps people to learn and communicate across different languages, as it always remains the same.

- Mathematics is often described by its branches: algebra, geometry, probability and statistics, and ratio and proportion.

- Early computers used binary systems—which use only zeros and ones as a code—and would only perform simple tasks.

- Scientific theories are often written as formulas, and basic arithmetic is used to collect and store data about the world around us.

- Math is often used to explain natural patterns found in the world around us, such as symmetry, fractals, spirals, and tessellations.

ANSWERS

LESSON 1: NUMBERS

ANSWER THIS

1.1 Numbers and Order

1. Twenty-two thousand, four hundred and sixty-five
2. d
3. c
4. odd

1.2 Negative Numbers

1. b
2. a
3. d

1.3 Decimals

1. c
2. d
3. c
4. 3.98, 3.982, 3.99, 4.02, 4.091, 4.1

1.4 Standard Form

1. 2×10^3
2. 5.721×10^7
3. 4×10^{-5}
4. 6.92×10^{-9}

1.5 Rounding and Estimation

1. b
2. a
3. a
4. d

1.6 Bounds

1. 2,025
2. 150
3. d

1.7 Factors, Multiples, and Primes

1. 1, 2, 3, 4, 6, 12
2. d
3. 9, 18, 27, 36, 45
4. b
5. a

1.8 Square and Cube Numbers

1. d
2. b
3. a
4. a

QUIZ TIME

1. a
2. 52, 72, 98, 99, 101, 111, 113, 129, 132, 146
3. d
4. b
5. c
6. 6.872×10^6
7. 900
8. d
9. 1, 24, 2, 12, 3, 8, 4, 6
10. b
11. c
12.

Number	Square number
1	1
2	4
3	**9**
4	16
5	**25**
6	**36**
7	49
8	**64**
9	**81**
10	100
11	**121**
12	**144**

LESSON 2: CALCULATIONS

ANSWER THIS

2.1 Adding and Subtracting

1. 5987
2. 101,987
3. 2813
4. 580
5. 97

2.2 Multiplying Without a Calculator

1. 102
2. 756
3. 216
4. 16,353

2.3 Dividing Without a Calculator

1. 12
2. 19 r 3 or $19^3/_4$
3. 52 r 3 or $52^3/_8$
4. 23 r 7 or $23^7/_{12}$
5. 422 r 1 or $422^1/_{22}$

2.4 Order of Operations

1. d
2. b
3. d
4. a

2.5 Doing Math in Your Head

1. 235
2. 370
3. 364
4. 521
5. 576

2.6 Multiplying by 10s, 100s, 1000s

1. a
2. d
3. c
4. d

2.7 Dividing by 10s, 100s, 1000s

1. b
2. c
3. c
4. a

2.8 Calculating with Money

1. $1.51
2. $150.26
3. c, as the small salad is $0.025 per g (2.50/100), the medium salad is $0.021 per g (4.20/200), and the large salad is $0.02 per g (10.00/500), making the large salad the cheapest per gram

QUIZ TIME

1. b
2. a
3. 133
4. 10,344
5. 28
6. 1458 r 4 or $1458^4/_5$
7. d
8. b
9. 453
10. 224
11. c
12. a
13. d
14. b
15. $10.25
16. b: The bag contains 5 pears and costs $5, that means each pear in the bag costs $1($5 ÷ 5 pears = $1 per pear). This is less than the individual pears, which cost $1.05, so is better value for money.

LESSON 3: DECIMALS, FRACTIONS, AND PERCENTAGES

ANSWER THIS

3.1 Introduction to Fractions

1. a
2. d
3. b
4. d

3.2 Mixed Numbers and Improper Fractions

1. $^{26}/_9$
2. $^{97}/_{12}$
3. $2^1/_5$
4. $7^7/_{11}$

3.3 Comparing Fractions

1. $^2/_{15}$
2. $^2/_6$, $^2/_5$, $^1/_2$, $^2/_3$
3. $^5/_9$ and $^{30}/_{54}$
4. $1^3/_7$, $1^5/_{11}$, $1^1/_2$

3.4 Adding and Subtracting Fractions

1. $^{11}/_{12}$
2. $^2/_5$
3. $1^{37}/_{56}$
4. $5^{67}/_{72}$

3.5 Multiplying and Dividing Fractions

1. $1^1/_3$
2. $^3/_{32}$
3. $^5/_{21}$
4. $2^1/_4$

3.6 Percentages

1. 25%
2. 12%
3. 84%
4. 64%

3.7 Converting Percentages into Fractions and Decimals

1. 23/100
2. 11/20
3. 0.39
4. 98%

3.8 Converting Fractions into Decimals

1. 0.03
2. 0.65
3. 0.375
4. 0.4444

QUIZ TIME

1. a
2. b

---

3. $^{47}/_{11}$
4. $7^4/_7$
5. a
6. $2^1/_6$, $2^2/_5$, $2^5/_9$
7. $3^{86}/_{99}$
8. $8^{13}/_{60}$
9. $^4/_{21}$
10. $^{28}/_{33}$
11. c
12. d
13. $^{16}/_{25}$
14. 0.37
15. 0.13
16. 0.22

LESSON 4: MEASUREMENTS

ANSWER THIS

4.1 What is Time?

1. 7:40 p.m.
2. 23:55
3. c

4.2 Units of Measurement

1. b
2. b
3. c
4. a

4.3 Imperial Units

1. 12 inches
2. 16 ounces
3. 3 yards
4. 5 gallons
5. 36 feet

4.4 Metric Units

1. a
2. c
3. 350 cm
4. 1.645 km
5. 4,300 g

4.5 Converting Units

1. Bertie, as 32 pounds is equal to 14.5 kg (or Alfie's weight of 13 kg is equal to 28.6 kg)
2. Redwood, as Mountain Ash is equal to 9,900 cm, which is 99 m, and, therefore, shorter (or Redwood is 383 feet)
3. 93°C

4.6 Perimeters

1. 12 inches (3 + 3 + 3 + 3 = 12 inches)
2. 30 inches (5 + 5 + 5 + 5 + 5 + 5 = 30)
3. 25.1 cm (π x 8)

4.7 Calculating and Estimating Areas

1. a
2. 49 in^2 (7 x 7 = 49)
3. 40 cm^2 (8 x 10 ÷ 2 = 40)
4. 254.5 ft^2 (9 x 9 = 81, 81 x π = 254.4690)

4.8 Calculating Volumes

1. 729 cm^3 (9 x 9 x 9)
2. 36 in^3 (6 x 3 x 2)
3. 113 ft^3 (3^3 x π x $^4/_3$)

QUIZ TIME

1. c
2. a
3. b
4. d
5. c
6. 4 pounds
7. 2,780 m
8. a
9. 512 in³
10. (i) P = 20 in A = 25 in²

(ii) P = 24 cm A = 27 cm²

(iii) P = 20 in A = 14 in²

(iv) C = 25.13 m A = 50.27 m²

LESSON 5: GEOMETRY: SHAPES, LINES, POINTS, ANGLES

ANSWER THIS

5.1 2-D Shapes

1. a

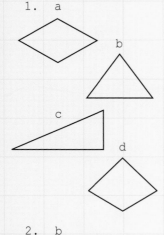

2. b

5.2 3-D Shapes

1. d
2. a
3. c

5.3 Shape Nets

1. Cone
2. Cube
3. Square-based pyramid
4. Triangular prism

5.4 Measuring and Identifying Angles

1. a
2. c
3. Corner of the angle
4. 90°, 180°

5.5 Geometry Rules

1. c
2. 90° (180 - 45 x 2)
3. b
4. 120° (360 - 40 - 90 - 110)

5.6 Lines of Symmetry

1. c
2. a
3. b

5.7 Angles in Parallel Lines

1. b
2. c

5.8 Bearings and Maps

1. Clockwise
2. b

QUIZ TIME

1. d
2. c
3. a
4. d
5. b
6. b
7. a
8. c
9. b
10. b

LESSON 6: RATE OF CHANGE, RATIO, AND PROPORTION

ANSWER THIS

6.1 Ratios

1. d
2. a
3. b
4. d

6.2 Conversions Using Ratios

1. 15 inches (3 x 5 = 15, as the height is now 5 times)
2. 2:4:2:2

6.3 Direct Proportion

1. $3.00 (1.80 ÷ 6 = 0.30, 0.30 × 10 = 3.00)
2. 2,555 miles (49 ÷ 7 = 7, 7 × 365 = 2,555)
3. 48 books (8 ÷ 2 = 4, 4 × 12 = 48)

6.4 Compound Growth and Decay

1. $275,625 (1st year: 5% of 250,000 is 12,500, so 250,000 + 12,500 = 262,500; 2nd year: 5% of 262,500 = 13,125, so 262,500 + 13,125 = 275,625)

2. $87.50 (1st year: 50% of 700 is 350, so 700 − 350 = 350; 2nd year: 50% of 350 is 175, so 350 − 175 = 175; 3rd year: 50% of 175 is 87.5)

6.5 Pressure, Force, Area

1. 7.5 Pa (30/4 = 7.5)
2. 50 psi (250/5 = 50)
3. 2 m² (8/4 = 2)
4. 35 pounds (10 x 3.5 = 35)

6.6 Percentage Change

1. d
2. c
3.a) 1.20
3.b) 12 flowers
4.a) 0.85
4.b) 34 pounds

6.7 Maps and Scale Drawings

1. 4 inches (1200/300 = 4)
2. 7 inches (49/7 = 7)
3. 10 km (5 x 2 = 10)

6.8 Density and Speed

1. 11.5 pounds/cubic foot (230/20 = 11.5)
2. 400 g (20 x 20 = 400)
3. 180 miles (60 x 3 = 180)
4. 0.5 miles/minute (7/14 = 0.5)

QUIZ TIME

1. a
2. d
3. c
4. c
5. d
6. a
7.a) 0.58
7.b) 145 leaves
8. b
9.

LESSON 7: ALGEBRA: WHEN MATH IS MORE THAN NUMBERS

ANSWER THIS

7.1 Using Symbols

1. d
2. b
3. a

7.2 Using and Writing Formulas

1. W = nR + B
2. A = ¹/₂₅ HB
3. T = 4 + 2n (T = total cost, n = number of drinks)

7.3 Using and Writing Expressions

1. x − 50 (he gained x but lost 50)
2. 10 + b
3. 200 ÷ t

7.4 Simplifying Terms

1. 3x + 4y
2. 11x
3. 9c − 8b + a
4. 24e² + 7e
5. 60x³

7.5 Multiplying Out Brackets

1. 30x + 6
2. 18y − 8z
3. 10z − 90

7.6 Factorizing

1. 2(y − 7)
2. 4(3x + 2)
3. x(x + 8)
4. y(y − 12)

7.7 Using Formulas to Solve Problems

1. 4 bottles of paint and 10 brushes
2. 6 bottles of paint and 5 brushes

7.8 Patterns and Sequences

1. Add 4 to the previous term
2. Subtract 9 from the previous term
3. Divide the previous term by 2
4. Subtract an extra 1 from the previous term
4. 81 (25 x 3 + 6)

QUIZ TIME

1. d
2. a
3. d
4. a
5. c
6. c
7. b
8. d
9.a) *Total = cost of table × number of tables + cost of chairs × number of chairs + cost of seat cushions × number of seat cushions*
9.b) $400 = 100t + 25c + 10s$
9.c) 8
10. Minus 8 from the previous term
11. a
12. Squared numbers

LESSON 8: STATISTICS AND PROBABILITY

ANSWER THIS

8.1 Probability

1. c
2. d

8.2 Counting Outcomes

1.a) 64 outcomes (2 x 2 x 2 x 2 x 2 x 2 = 64)
1.b) 0.02 (1 ÷ 64 = 0.0156…)
2.a) 1,296 (6 x 6 x 6 x 6 = 1,296)
2.b) 0.06 (3 x 3 x 3 x 3 = 81, 81/1296 = 1/16)

8.3 Probability It Won't Happen

1. d
2. 5/6 or 0.833
3. c

8.4 Probability Experiments

1. a
2. c

8.5 The And/Or Rules

1. d
2. 0.33 (4/12 = 0.3333)
3. a (P(4) = 0.1666 and P(tails) = 0.5, P(4) and P(tails = 0.16666 x 0.5 = 0.083

8.6 Tree Diagrams

1. $^{16}/_{49}$ [working out: $^4/_7 \times ^4/_7$]
2. $^{12}/_{49}$ [working out: $^3/_7 \times ^3/_7$]
3. $^{25}/_{49}$ [working out: $^4/_7 \times ^4/_7 + ^3/_7 \times ^3/_7$]

8.7 Conditional Probability

1. a [working out: $^9/_{12} \times ^3/_{11}$]
2. c [working out: $^9/_{12} \times ^8/_{11} \times ^3/_{12} \times ^2/_{11}$]

8.8 Sets and Venn Diagrams

1. {1, 4, 9, 16, 25, 36, 49, 64, 81, 100}
2. $^{23}/_{25}$

QUIZ TIME

1. a
2. b
3. d
4. b
5. c
6. b
7.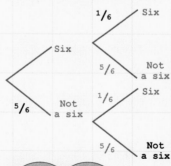
8.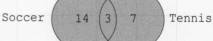

LESSON 9: GRAPHS: PRESENTING DATA IN THE BEST WAY

ANSWER THIS

9.1 Presenting Data in Tables

1.

Morning lessons schedule

	Sarah	Jennifer	Hannah
9:00	English	English	Math
10:00	Math	Art	Geography
11:00	Spanish	Art	Spanish
12:00	Lunch	Lunch	Lunch

9.2 Schedules and Timetables

1. d
2. c
3. b
4. d

9.3 Bar Charts

1. c
2. b
3. a

9.4 Pictograms

1. b
2. a
3.
4. c

9.5 Scattergraphs

1. a
2. b
3. b

9.6 Line Graphs

1. b
2. b
3. c
4. a

9.7 Pie Charts

1. a
2. c
3. b
4. d

9.8 Averages: Mean, Mode, Median

1.a) 63, 63, 64, 64, 64, 64, 64, 65, 65, 65, 65, 67, 67, 68, 69
1.b) 65°F
1.c) 64°F
1.d) 65.1°F (977/15 = 65.1)

QUIZ TIME

1.(i) 25 minutes
1.(ii) 8:37

2. Monday
   Tuesday
   Wednesday
   Thursday
   Friday
3. c
4.(i)   4 ounces
4.(ii) 5 ounces
4.(iii) 5.8 ounces

LESSON 10: ORIGINS AND USE OF MATH

ANSWER THIS

10.1 History of Early Mathematics

1. b
2. d
3. Geometric
4. a

10.2 Math in Modern Life

1. b
2. c

10.3 Problem-solving Skills

1. d
2. a
3. b

10.4 Universal Language

1. b
2. a
3. d
4. a

10.5 Symbols and Concepts

1. a
2. a
3. b
4. c

10.6 Mathematics and Computing

1. Zero and one
2. 1111
3. B

10.7 Mathematics in Science

1. Physics
2. Formulas or equations
3. Statistics

10.8 Mathematics in Nature

1. c
2. a
3. b
4. d

QUIZ TIME

1. b
2. c
3. b
4. b
5. a
6. c
7. b
8. d
9.a) Tessellation
9.b) Symmetry (specifically, bilateral)

GLOSSARY

Algebra The use of symbols and letters in place of numbers to create formulas, equations, and expressions.

Area How much space a shape occupies, measured in squared units, i.e. inches squared (in^2) or centimeters squared (cm^2).

Average Number that summarizes data and can help with comparisons of other groups of data; can refer to mean, mode, or median.

Bearings Angles used in navigation, measured clockwise from the North line.

Correlation Relationship between two variables, can be positive or negative.

Factor Whole number that divides exactly into the original number.

Formula Mathematical rule or relationship written in symbols or letters.

Geometry The part of math dedicated to the size, shape, dimensions, and angles of objects.

Graph Way of presenting data that makes comparisons between sets easier to see.

Improper fraction Where the numerator (the number on top of a fraction) is larger than the denominator (on the bottom).

Mixed number Combination of a whole number and a fraction together.

Multiple Value in an original number's times table.

Number sequence Lists of numbers that follow a particular pattern.

Perimeter The distance around the outside of a 2-D shape (known as circumference in circles).

Polyhedron Three-dimensional shape with flat sides.

Pressure Measure of how much force is applied over a given area, measured in Pascals (Pa) or psi.

Prime number	A number that only has two factors: itself and 1.
Probability	Chance or likelihood of something occurring.
Product	Total value when multiplying two or more numbers together.
Proportion	How amounts are related to one another.
Ratio	Relationship between two or more amounts.
Regular polygon	2-D shape with equal-length sides and angles, such as a square.
Shape net	2-D shape that makes a 3-D shape when folded.
Square number	The product of that number multiplied by itself twice.
Statistics	Analysis of numerical data to see if there are relationships.
Sum	Total value of an addition of two or more numbers.
Term	A letter, symbol, or number (or combination thereof) on its own within a formula.
Volume	The amount of 3-D space a shape takes up, measured in cubed units, i.e. inches cubed (in^3) or centimeters cubed (cm^3).

FURTHER READING

BOOKS:

All the Math You'll Ever Need: A Self-Teaching Guide Revised Edition
Steve Slavin
(Wiley, 1999)

Design a Skyscraper (You Do the Math)
Hilary Koll & Steve Mills
(QEP Publishing, 2015)

Difficult Riddles For Smart Kids: 300 Difficult Riddles And Brain Teasers Families Will Love
M. Prefontaine
(CreateSpace Independent Publishing Platform, 2017)

Every Day Math Practice: 1000+ Questions You Need to Kill in Middle School
Brian Hunter Prep
(Brian Hunter Prep Inc., 2018)

Everything You Need to Ace Math in One Big Fat Notebook: The Complete Middle School Study Guide
Altair Peterson
(Workman Publishing Company, 2016)

Football: The Math of the Game (Sports Math)
Shane Frederick
(Capstone Press, 2011)

It's a Numberful World: How Math Is Hiding Everywhere
Eddie Wood
(The Experiment LLC, 2018)

Math Adventures with Python: An Illustrated Guide to Exploring Math with Code
Peter Farrell
(No Starch Press, 2019)

Math Art: Truth, Beauty, and Equations
Stephen Ornes
(Sterling, 2019)

Math Dictionary for Kids: The #1 Guide for Helping Kids With Math
Theresa Fitzgerald
(Prufrock Press, 2016)

Math Doesn't Suck: How to Survive Middle School Math Without Losing Your Mind or Breaking a Nail
Danica McKellar
(Plume, 2008)

Math Fact Fluency: 60+ Games and Assessment Tools to Support Learning and Retention
Jennifer Bay-Williams & Gina Kling
(ASCD, 2019)

Math Puzzles Volume 1: Classic Riddles and Brain Teasers In Counting, Geometry, Probability, and Game Theory
Presh Talwalkar
(CreateSpace Independent Publishing Platform, 2015)

Math with Bad Drawings: Illuminating the Ideas That Shape Our Reality
Ben Orlin
(Black Dog & Leventhal, 2018)

My Best Mathematical and Logic Puzzles
Martin Gardner
(Dover Publications, 1994)

Perfectly Logical!: Challenging Fun Brain Teasers and Logic Puzzles for Smart Kids
Jenn Larson
(Zephyros Press, 2019)

Secrets of Mental Math: The Mathemagician's Guide to Lightning Calculation and Amazing Math Tricks
Arthur Benjamin & Michael Shermer
(Three Rivers Press, 2006)

The Book of Perfectly Perilous Math: 24 Death-Defying Challenges for Young Mathematicians
Sean Connolly
(Workman Publishing Company, 2012)

The Magic of Math: Solving for x and Figuring Out Why
Arthur Benjamin
(Basic Books, 2016)

The Math Book: From Pythagoras to the 57th Dimension, 250 Milestones in the History of Mathematics
Clifford A. Pickover
(Sterling, 2012)

WEBSITES:
GeoGebra
www.geogebra.org

Illuminations (National Council of Teachers of Mathematics)
https://illuminations.nctm.org

Khan Academy
www.khanacademy.org

Math Help
www.mathhelp.com

PBS Math Club
www.pbslearningmedia.org/collection/pbs-math-club

INDEX

CREDITS

First, I want to thank my Dad, Malcolm, for passing on his passion for math and science; and my Mom, Christine, for listening to me talk about math nonstop! I am also grateful to my nephew, Jack, for his helpful discussions on math topics. Thank you Dexter, for being by my side throughout the whole researching and writing process, and my sister, Helen, for the use of your extremely quiet, and therefore not distracting, house. Lastly, I would also like to thank my publishing team, Abbie and Katie, for giving me the opportunity to put my passion for math education into print.

Images:
Unless otherwise noted, all images have been created by Tall Tree.

Shutterstock: 9, 28, 48, 68, 88, 108, 128, 148, 168, 188, 208, 210 Blan-k; 15 jkcDesign; 17 Babich Alexander; 19 TheBestGraphics; 23 gst; 40 HYDNSTUDIO, Sansom.C; 46 Jane Kelly; 47 olllikeballoon; 56 Vova_31; 60 Sudowoodo; 60, 86, 137 yayha; 62 Dmytro 007; 63 gasa, MvanCaspel; 65 Sansom.C; 72 Uncle Leo; 73 tovovan; 74 gomolach, Yanas; 75 Vecton, Adecvatman; 77 Ollivka; 78 Anatolir; 81 ahmad agung wijayanto; 82 yayha; 86 Simvector, bungacengkeh; 98 Natsmith1; 106–107 paseven; 107 elmm; 112 ClassicVector, Zita; 113 peart, Hein Nouwens; 115 BigMouse; 116 Rvector; 119–120 Vectors Bang, studioworkstock; 122 Lole; 124 VectorsMarket; 124-125 Eugene Ga; 125 Handies Peak; 134 PannaKotta; 136 AbdulrhmanZaki, pear worapan; 144 Zonda, Glinskaja Olga, Vectorpocket, Macrovector; 154 Paper Teo; 155 Adam Fahey Designs; 156 unknown contributor (toys), peart, Vikivector; 157 peart; 157, 160, 163 Senoldo; 159 Mastal Inc; 160-161 Vector Walker; 165 mything, Anait, Blablo101, 178, 216 Vector Tradition; 179 NataLima; 186 sabri deniz kizil; 194 VectorHot; 196 studioworkstock; 197 gst, N.D. Fernandez; 198 Lana2016; 204 elyomys; 206 Platonova Sveta, Alhovik, artyway, Shanvood.